Crystal Skillman and Fred Van Lente

KING KIRBY

Please direct inquiries about production rights to: Amy Wagner & Ronald Gwiazda at Abrams Artists Agency, 275 Seventh Ave., 26th Floor New York, NY 10001 amy.wagner@abramsartny.com // ron.gwiazda@abramsartny.com

Amazing Fantasy, The Amazing Spider-Man, Bucky, Captain America, *Captain America Comics,* Dragon Man, *Fantastic Four,* Galactus, The Hulk, Inhumans, Iron Man, Invisible Girl, Silver Surfer, *Thor, X-Men,* and, presumably, Mr. Liberty and United States Man, are TM and © Marvel Characters, Inc.

Batman, Blue Beetle, *Boy Commandos, New Gods,* Superman, Wonder Woman and *Young Romance* are TM and © DC Comics.

Popeye is TM and © Hearst Holdings, Inc.

This play, though inspired by fact, is a work of fiction.

Cover art by Ryan Dunlavey.

Kickstarter Backers' Edition, August 2014 • Published by the authors

The 2014 Comic Book Theater Festival Production of ***King Kirby*** could not have been possible without the generosity of our Kickstarter backers. Thank you, one and all.

A.J. Magoon
Adam McGovern
Adrienne
Alexa Antopol
Alfredo Ignacio
Amr El-Wakeel
Amy Chu
Andragana I.A.
Andrew Sanford
Ann Sedman
Annie Hall
Avri Klemer
Ben Cohen
Ben Miller
Ben Pyle
Bob Cairns
Brandon
Brandon Lori
Brent Stringer
Brett Monro
Brett Simon
Brian Macken
Brian Schirmer
brownbagcomics
Carla
Carlos Jonay
   Suárez Suárez
Carol Holsinger
Chaotic Geek
Charles Soule
Chris Allingham
Chris Nolan.ca
Chris Schoenthal
Chris Sims
Chris Suggs
Chris Vincent
Chriss Cornish
Christian Berntsen

Christopher Greer
Christopher
   Northern
Christopher Todd
   Kjergaard
Ciaran Downey
Cindy Womack
Cody Robison
Constantine
   Koutsoutis
Cory Smith
Daniel Drew Turner
Daniel McGowan
Daniel Newman
Dannimals
David Burszan
David Cilley
David G Bernstein
David Gossett
David Macpherson
David Wellington
Dean Haspiel
Derrick Sanskrit
Devon Devereaux
Dog Days Films
Don MacDonald
Donald Claxon
Doug Triplett
Dr. Alexander Bustos
Dr. Fred & Beth Van
   Lente
Drew Tynan Robbins
Ed Barton
Ed Garrett
EJ Feddes
Ellen Abramowitz
Eric Damon Walters
Eric Owens

Evil Twin Comics
Father-Funk
Frank Barbiere
Frederik Hautain
Gary Arkell
Geoffrey Sproule
Ghoulash Games
Greg Pak
Hannah Rothman
Harley Jebens
Jack Kirby Museum
   & Research Center
Jacob Bihl
James Asmus
James Tynion IV
Jamie Tanner
Janna O'Shea
Jarrett Melendez
Jeff Metzner
Jeremy Weathers
Jesse Farrell
Jesse W. [w5748]
Jim Berry
Jim Gibbons
Joe Caramagna
Joe Corallo
Joe Dallacqua
Joel Carlson
Joey
Joey Esposito
John Anderson
John Carr
John Falcon
John S. Troutman
John Sanders
John Stirrat
Jonathan Voris
Joseph Konsouls

3

Josh Maher
Josh Sinason
Josh Young
Joshua Dover
Joshua Lazarus
Julian Chambliss
K. David Marple
Karl Endebrock
Kathrin Brogli
Kelly Luce
Kenny Porter
Kevin J. Maroney
Kevin Walker
Leah Spano
Lee Ferguson
Liam Dinneen
Łukasz Bury
Lyle Tucker
Lynne Lipton
Marc Jones
Mark Coale
Markee Games
Mat Elfring
Mathew Groom
Matthew Barr
Matthew Cranor
Matthew
    Weinberger
Megan Kingery
metagnat
Michael Abbott
Michael Cotey
Michael Eckett
Michael Levis
Michael Perlman
Mike McGee
Mike Norton
Mike Ortiz
Mike Weiss
Miriam Barberena

mkobar
Mo Kristiansen
multitudrops
Natan Skop
Nate Cosby
Nathan Leatherman
Nathan Slavec
Nathanael Pine
Nick Dragotta
Noah
Patrick Barb
Patrick Curry
Patrick Hess
Patty Marvel
pauldesmond
Pere Pérez Pérez
Phil Hester
Philip and Johanna
    Vandrey
Philip Uebbing
Playlab NYC
Prestond
Prodigal
Rafer Roberts
Ray Ghanbari
Reza Tootoonchian
Rich Burlew
Richard Gotlib
Richard Lemon
Richard Meehan
Robbie Dorman
Robert Altherr
Robert Jarvis
Robert Rosenthal
Robin Harman
Roshan Abraham
Ruben Bolling
Russell & Marie
    Skillman
Ryan Wilson

SamuraiGodZilla
Sean Arnold
SecretGG
Shani Harris
Shannon Spurlock
Sharmini
Steve Meyer
Steve Siwy
Steven Smith
Sunny Raj N
Taimur Dar
Tamisha Hopkins
Tara Bruno
TC
Ted Delorme
Thomas O'Hagan
Tim
Tim Seeley
Todd Dixon
Tom Critchlow
Tony Fleecs
Topher Davila
Tor Andre
Wigmostad
Trevor
Tyler Swanger
Valentí Acconcia
    González
Van Jensen
Vera Greentea
Victoria Elizabeth-
    Francis De Maria
Wade Woodson
WIARLAWD
William Sliney
Zachariah
Dominello
zgneishik
[insertgeekhere]

"It's not created by a machine – it's art created by people" – An Interview with *King Kirby* Playwrights Crystal Skillman and Fred Van Lente
by Reid Vanier

In *King Kirby*, the life of iconic comic book creator Jack Kirby makes its theatrical debut as part of the 2014 Comic Book Theater Festival in New York City. Leading up to its opening on June 20, playwrights Crystal Skillman and Fred Van Lente took some time to discuss the legacy of Kirby's life in comics, the theatrical process, and the Kickstarter campaign that's helping to bring the story to life.

Hello Crystal and Fred. It is very clear to me from reading about this project that you both have a tremendous love and respect for Jack Kirby. How did that relationship begin? Do you remember your first introductions to his work?

Crystal: Bizarrely enough, I realized when talking to the other day – the first day I realized who Jack was I was watching *Superman: The Animated Series* in 1998!

Fred and I had been together since '96, and I very much loved graphic novels. I was lucky enough to see the MOMA show of Art Spiegelman's *Maus!* So to me there was no doubt that comics were art and art was comics and I just loved them.

While dating Fred in those early days I was getting to know a whole new world of comics just by getting to know his close friends – Ryan Dunlavey, Steve Ellis and Jamal Igle! Just by coming over I was getting brought into this world by watching them all create.

Of course, when not creating most of us would be watching cartoons! When I saw the death of the character Dan Turpin on the series (the character was based on how Kirby looked), I saw at the end that the episode was dedicated to Jack Kirby.

When I asked about Kirby, it was clear even in speaking about his work that Fred and his friends had such a passion for his work. I also realized many of the characters I was seeing in those Superman episodes, dealing with the Fourth World and Darkseid, were some of my favorite characters I'd seen.

I picked up *New Gods* and started to realize the influence of Kirby on comics, the art world, and pop culture in general. It's astounding how I didn't know his name until then. That always stuck with me.

Are there aspects of your interest in comics that were inspired or bolstered by Kirby's influence?

Crystal: For sure, the impact Kirby has had on comic book creators today is amazing. There in that little house on Webster Place in Brooklyn, I was seeing it among Fred's friends − their passion and reverence for Kirby. Not unlike, I'd say, how we talk about some of our play-writing greats who broke through, and their influences on my generation − Tony Kushner, Caryl Churchill, Susan Lori Parks, David Henry Hwang, Lynn Notage, to name a few.

And Fred, how did the "King of Comics" specifically affect your career trajectory in the comics industry?

Fred: I started out as a kid reading '70s reprints of the Marvel work, then as a college student I encountered *New Gods* for the first time and it blew me away.

The sense of adventure, the infectious inventiveness − all this has infused my own work in the superhero genre. I'm one of these guys who's often described as making "fun" comics; I don't see how that'd be possible without Kirby's influence.

Fans are most familiar with Kirby's "product": the characters and comic books that are now the foundation of his artistic legacy. Without giving too much away, how incomplete is that portrait of the man?

Crystal: Even in talking about the show with those outside of comics, the urgency and need to tell Jack's story has become pretty clear. While Kirby is known in comics circles, his name doesn't really ring a bell with those unfamiliar with comics, but his images do.

Every time I talked about our play to those outside of the comics industry, friends immediately said – "Ohhhh, like that book – *The Adventures of Kavalier & Clay!*" Most folks didn't realize that the world and events created in Michael Chabon's novel were inspired by much of Jack's life.

That happened so often, I use it myself now as a touchstone when talking about the play. *But* when you saw Kirby's artwork – it's instantly recognizable. Much of our play is an investigation of how could that happen? As Fred has been saying, do people know where their pop culture comes from? It's not created by a machine – it's art created by people.

In getting to know the artist behind the image, suddenly you're in the middle of a whole other story. Luckily there are so many interviews with Jack, there is much to access on his feelings of the events of his life. But of course, some of his thoughts contradict each other. Which, for a dramatist, is exciting.

The play asks "Who is the creator of a story?" In his life, Kirby's fight to be known as a creator, and to work on his own characters, is an inspirational one for artists because it brings up a great point; if an artist *draws* the story – in comics, which is a marriage of words and pictures – isn't that just as important as the writer of the script?

Similarly, I imagine that Kirby's close association with the comic medium presents its own challenges when developing the story for the theatre. What was the inspiration to tell this story theatrically? Moreover, how do you approach the story theatrically while still making it recognizably Jack Kirby?

Crystal: What makes the play unique to me is you're following several key players, growing from the very birth of comics as its own medium over several years. Honestly, there's a real wonderful *Glengarry Glen Ross* feel in the offices scenes – only with comic book creators.

You really feel like a fly on the wall watching how Kirby creates and struggles with these office politics. For many, I think they'll feel like they're getting to go "backstage" in some ways and really get not only how the comics industry was formed, but also the amount of joy, pain, sweat, and tears that goes into creating a comic book.

The play for sure follows Kirby and his own investigation of his life. We show more how the events in his life affected his style. So there's a very grounded sensibility to that portrayal. But in that style, in terms of theatrics, there is a real heightened sense to the story we're seeing unfold on stage.

In the writing, I think Fred did a terrific job of capturing the frenetic energy of Kirby. John Hurley has a wonderful theatrical style to his direction and he captures this dynamic energy really well with the actors and his staging.

Steven Rattazzi, a brilliant actor who readers might know as Dr. Orpheus on *Venture Brothers*, has created a Kirby that is really unique, I think. He captures the spirit and drive of Jack, while allowing us to hear his inner thoughts on what he's discovering in this most incredible life ...

When writing this kind of work, as I discovered in my play Geek, set at an animation convention, it's important to identify with the character in this journey, then build the fantasy out from there. Kirby is our way into the play, and that distinction is important.

The play opens at one of the greatest crises of Kirby's life – after his death. The Sotheby's auction of his work. We know what's at stake, what has been lost, but how? The play dives into that question and, along the way, Kirby questions his own choices.

All I know is that I helped Fred work on it, I know the story, and I'm still engrossed at every rehearsal. It's a really unique play in how it engages with telling the story of such an important figure in history. We're so excited to share this play with an audience.

Working together on this project, you are both a literal and figurative marriage of the two different art forms. Has the collaborative process produced any major surprises for either of you? Is there any particular discovery that stands out?

Crystal: One of the greatest joys was discovering how much Fred loves rehearsal! What makes theater so unique and such a joy is that the words and actions you write come to life right there in front of you.

Rehearsal is all about creating the beats in a play that we'll see unfold – how the conflicts climax and bring us to a new place of discovery as an audience. Being there as a writer, in the room, with actors making that come to life, is a very exciting experience. For me, after having several productions, it's wonderful to see a writer as accomplished as Fred discovering this joy. Through his eyes, it's reminded me about what I love about creating live theater.

As for a specific discovery, in early drafts, while we saw scenes with Stan, there was no final confrontation. When working on the play, I knew this moment had to happen, but how it happens must be truthful to history and also to both sides, as there are such different viewpoints. I wrote a draft of that scene, which Fred only made stronger in a rewrite. It's very moving and true about the art of creation.

When I came into rehearsal a bit late the other day, John was blocking the last scene of the play. It was so moving I felt myself getting choked up. I think we're onto something universal, truthful and real. To me, that's what I love about theater. We want to see characters bare their soul; in a way, it liberates us to think about our own lives.

I might feel so passionately about this as I lost a great playwright and very close friend, John Belluso. While his plays are still performed, his identity and who he was seems to be lost to a new generations of writers. While I hope in the future to correct that in some way, it creates a feeling of helplessness. It strikes a chord. What will people take away from our work when we're gone?

Of course, I'd like to call attention to the "King Kirby" Kickstarter campaign. Obviously you are seeking support for the production of the play, but it feels like a very inviting gesture as well – a chance for other fans to contribute to Kirby's legacy. In this way, crowdfunding the show feels thematically relevant. Was that a deliberate artistic consideration?

Crystal: Fred's done an amazing job of putting this together. He really saw this as being about communicating our work together as artists, about spreading the word of how important the story of Jack Kirby is, to those who love him or are getting to know him for the first time.

I think the Kickstarter campaign and how it's growing really hits home how artists can fight to keep sharing their own work – even if they must do it independently!

Finally, what are your ultimate hopes for this play? Does it have a specific future after this initial run?

Crystal: That's my hope! I recently as in Seattle recently hearing my play, *Another Kind of Love*, about a family of punk rock stars, in a great reading with LiveGirls!, a theater out there. Everyone kept asking me about the play! Some real Kirby fans!

It's clear to me that the play would really be exciting for communities around the globe to hear; I hope it'll find homes in many more theaters and allow as many fans, and those getting to know Jack for the first time, to keep pondering what it means to create – and why do we keep doing it?

It's a pretty inspiring story as well. Jack was always about the next project, the next thing. While his life as a creator was a struggle, that spark is a wonderful thing to investigate – and to make sure it keeps burning in our own lives and work.

*This article originally appeared on the web site **Broken Frontier** on June 19, 2014 (http://www.brokenfrontier.com).*

King Kirby was initially presented at The Brick Theater in Brooklyn, New York, on June 20, 2014 in conjunction with the 2014 Comic Book Theater Festival. It was directed by John Hurley; set and lighting design by Olivia Harris; costume design by Holly Rihn; sound design by Janie Ballard. The cast was as follows:

Kirby	Steven Rattazzi
Simon (and others)	Joseph Mathers
Fox (and others)	Timothy McCown Reynolds
Stanley (and others)	Nat Cassidy
Roz (and others)	Amy Lee Pearsall

Cast Breakdown of (Non-Kirby) Roles

Actress
Auctioneer
Suffolk 1
Union Organizer
Comic Book Artist 1
Crank Caller
Sexy Secretary
Roz
Industry Flak
New Journalist

Actor 1
Ludlow 1
Dispatcher
Animator 2
Joe Simon
German Soldier
Student 1
Fan 1

Actor 2
Ludlow 2
Spaceman
Kirby's Dad
Animator 3
Comic Book Artist 2
Radio Announcer
Stanley/Stan Lee
Corporal
Lieutenant
Chairman Langer
Fan 2

Actor 3
Ludlow 3
Super
Animator 1
Victor Fox
Martin Goodman
Jack Liebowitz
Patton
Dr. Wertham
Student 2
Fellini

TIME & PLACE: *The play spans from 1929 to 1994 and several locations, most notably New York City, with side sojourns to California and France.*

SET: *Should be fluid and able to move easily. A simple, non-naturalistic, imaginative set is called for using light and sound to evoke setting and time in our imaginations.*

Though inspired by fact, this play is a work of fiction.

(Photo: Crystal Skillman)

Sotheby's Auction House, Manhattan. June 18, 1994.

As the audience enters, KIRBY is at his drawing desk, working feverishly, his back to us. He mutters to himself as he works.

A female AUCTIONEER at a lectern on an empty stage. She raps her gavel to get the audience's attention.

AUCTIONEER. *(British accent)* We'd like to get started, so if it everyone could take their seats, that would be wonderful. Thank you.

She waits for the audience to silence.

KIRBY. A spark makes a universe.

AUCTIONEER. Welcome to Sotheby's annual auction of comic book art and comic book related items. We are especially lucky today to have on hand several originals from the legendary cartoonist Jack Kirby, generally regarded by fans and collectors as *(finger quotes)* "The King of the Comics."

KIRBY. An idea makes a spark.

AUCTIONEER. Mister Kirby's recent death has driven up the value of much of his work, and if you look in your programs you'll see our appraiser's updated prices reflect that.

KIRBY. It comes into this real world — fighting.

AUCTIONEER. Our first item is Mr. Kirby's reproduction of the pencils to the cover to *Amazing Fantasy #15*. First appearance of the superhero Iron Man. *(checks notes)* Spider-Man. Pardon me. Spider-Man. I must confess — shockingly — I am not a comic book fan myself. I don't let them in the house, frankly. My boys fight enough as it is. But clearly — even if this isn't "art" in the traditional sense—

KIRBY. Haw!

AUCTIONEER. —it is a valuable piece of Americana, and the bidding will begin at—

KIRBY. That's enough! Don't wanna hear that number. Nothing's worse than hearing what you're worth after you're gone.

AUCTIONEER. *(raps gavel)* Sold! To the young man in the anorak.

KIRBY. Ideas create universes. Create characters. Story.

AUCTIONEER. Next up are the pencils to Mister Kirby's cover to *Fantastic Four #1*, the very first appearances of... *(can't find the characters' names on her sheet)*... those characters. From the movie.

KIRBY. But how a character finishes isn't up to him—

AUCTIONEER. Now, remember, even though this is commercial illustration, and the artist has largely subtracted himself from the work to appease the marketplace, unlike the purity of a Rembrandt or a Matisse, these are still historically significant works.

KIRBY. —any more than how he begins.

AUCTIONEER. So we have set bidding to begin at—

"I must confess — shockingly — I am not a comic book fan myself." (Photo: Crystal Skillman)

Kirby stands from his drawing table, silencing the Auctioneer as lights fade on her.

KIRBY. You're supposed to grow up. Learn the world isn't divided into heroes and villains. But that never happened to me. From the day I was born... They were all I could see.

The SOUNDS of the JEWISH GHETTO rise.

SCENE 2.

Suffolk Street, Lower East Side. 1929.

KIRBY. Later Nervous Nellies would say all that superhero stuff was too violent. Are you kidding me? Did you grow up on Suffolk Street, Lower East Side? It was like the farm team for the Mafia. Wait, no — not "like." It *was* the farm team for the Mafia.

Kirby joins the JEWISH BOYS preparing to do battle with IRISH KIDS from Ludlow Street.

KIRBY. Suffolk Street Jewish kids were always having to beat back the Irish-Catholics over on Ludlow!

IRISH KIDS. *Y'LICE! Y'LICE! C'MOUT, Y'LICE!*

LUDLOW #1. *CHRIST-KILLERS!*

SUFFOLK #1. *POTATO FARTS!*

LUDLOW #1. Gonna yank down your drawers and make sure you're circumcised, kike!

SUFFOLK #1. Your mother found out last night, Paddy!

LUDLOW #1. You hymie jew piece o' shit! You talking about my mother? I'm gonna cut off the rest of it!

The boys FREEZE right before they launch themselves at each other:

KIRBY. I liked fighting! It let me express my creativity! I used to take the train to different parts of town to pick fights, just to see different styles in different parts of town.

21

Kirby walks up to a kid, pushes him. They brawl; Kirby gets the upper hand, knocks him flat.

KIRBY. Not bad. Better uppercut than Ozone Park, but your dodging and weaving has got nothing on Flatbush. I'd give Hell's Kitchen, uh, a five. Out of ten.

THUNDERCLAP — a rainstorm. Some guy in an umbrella passes flips through a pulp magazine. He tosses it into a gutter. Kirby rushes past, holding a school book over his head, and sees it.

Running home from school in the rain when I first saw it, rushing past me in the gutter. I couldn't have been much more than ten. I saved it just before it got swept into the storm drain!

Kirby picks up the pulp magazine and flips through the pages.

A pulp magazine— *Science Wonder Stories.* On the cover— A rocket ship, blasting toward the moon! Spacemen, with ray guns, in shiny plastic space suits! Between the covers— Escape! Into stories— such stories! Pirates fighting aliens on the moons of Saturn! How could a kid resist? There it was, for the first time — the spark!

Kirby sketches picture stories on the floor with chalk. He mouths along with the character's lines, acting them out as he draws:

DISPATCHER. Attention Solar Legion! Fort Roosevelt destroyed by rocket cruisers of unknown identity! Scout units in Ursus Major ordered to inspect all ships in that sector!

SPACEMAN. Roaring rockets! Fort Roosevelt wiped out! I'll bet my wings it was Elramis and her cutthroats! If I spot that she-wolf and her mangy crew, I'll blast them clear to— Uh-oh! Ray flashes!

KIRBY. And there was something— Something where there used to be Nothing!

The building's SUPER enters.

"Escape! Into stories— such stories!" (Photo: Crystal Skillman)

SUPER. What the hell is this? You little pisher! You've covered the third floor landing with your facacta chalk drawings!

KIRBY. Go stick your ass in the sewer, you old cockroach! We can't afford paper!

SUPER. Let's see what your father says about that!

(going off)

Kurtzberg!

KIRBY. Shit.

Kirby turns to go but runs smack into his FATHER, Benjamin Kurtzberg, who has entered behind him. He grabs the piece of chalk from him.

KIRBY. I'm sorry dad, I just—

KIRBY'S DAD. I know Jakie.

KIRBY. I got all these ideas in my head.

KIRBY'S DAD. Outer space stuff again, huh? You know what they say if you fill your head with that garbage.

KIRBY. No.

KIRBY'S DAD. Me neither. Whoah! What's happening here?

KIRBY. This spaceguy is fighting that spaceguy and this one's saying: Roaring rockets! Blast 'em!

KIRBY'S DAD. I don't see any words.

KIRBY. Drawing's faster. You mad?

Kirby's dad gives him the piece of chalk back.

KIRBY'S DAD. I'll just stay here a while. Watch you finish if you don't... *(yawns)*

"Drawing's faster.." (Photo: Crystal Skillman)

Kirby draws.

KIRBY. He used to come in and just sit. So tired. How they used him in that sweatshop on Delancey, spitting out rags. Twelve hours days. Working, working.

What would appear to be a sweatshop is formed around him, a factory like the one his father worked in.

KIRBY. I was supposed to become him. I almost did.

Kirby pockets the chalk.

Fleischer Studios, Times Square. 1937.

KIRBY. My father got fired from his job working that sewing machine the day I was supposed to enter Pratt on an art scholarship.

The "factory" is actually an animation studio. Animators are at workbenches drawing Fleischer "Popeye" cartoons.

KIRBY. In the middle of the Depression, I get the first art job I applied for. Unfortunately.

Kirby sits at the center drawing table and begins working.

ANIMATORS. *(signing)* "I'm Popeye the Sailor Man, I'm Popeye the Sailor Man! I'm strong to the finich, cause I eats me spinach! I'm Popeye the Sailor Man!"

ANIMATOR #1. Annoying motherfucker ain't he. You're gonna have to be stronger than him to be an in-betweener.

KIRBY. We just draw the movement that connects key frames in a scene. No biggie, right?

ANIMATOR #1. Just wait til ya do it over and over and —

Over this, the animators pass drawings to each other in mechanical fashion, drawing for a few seconds, then passing the page along in mindless precision.

KIRBY. Say the first key frame was Popeye whipping out a can of spinach, and the next was him dumping the spinach in his mouth. My job would be to draw Popeye lifting the can at a ten degree angle... eleven degree angle... twelve...

thirteen...*(stops and stares at drawing) JUST EAT THE FUCKING SPINACH ALREADY!!*

ANIMATORS.*(singing angrily)* "I'm Popeye the Sailor Man, I live in the frying pan! I turned up the gas and blew off my ass, I'm Popeye the Sailor Man!"

KIRBY. I might as well be running a frickin' sewing machine like my father!

One of the animators, a UNION ORGANIZER, suddenly stands up from her drawing table.

UNION ORGANIZER. Brother workers! Where are your pensions? Where are your vacations? Local 20239 of the Commercial Artists' and Designers' Union has come to rescue you! We already broke the backs of the fat cats at Disney, in Hollywood! Why should New York be immune? Rise up! Seize the means of production! Strike! *STRIKE! STRIKE!*

ANIMATORS. *STRIKE! STRIKE! STRIKE!*

All except Kirby pick up placards that read things like "CAN'T MAKE MUCH SPINACH ON $15 A WEEK" and "I MAKE MILLIONS LAUGH BUT THE REAL JOKE IS OUR SALARIES."

ANIMATOR #1. C'mon, Jack, join us! The lines stretch from Broadway to Seventh Avenue!

KIRBY. Shows how much you know! You know who's behind the Commercial Artists' and Designers' Union? The Longshoremen! I grew up with these guys. Lansky's boys! Mobsters!

UNION ORGANIZER. Hey! Key animators are trying to enter the studio!

ANIMATOR #1. They said they'd stand with the in-betweeners!

"Annoying motherfucker ain't he." (Photo: Crystal Skillman)

UNION ORGANIZER. *HOLD THE LINE BOYS! DON'T LET THE SCABS IN! WE OUTNUMBER THE COPS 10-TO-1!*

Union Organizer and Animator #1 lock arms. A Key Animator tries to break through, but their line holds fast. A scuffle ensues.

KIRBY. Time to try a different industry! Where you going?

ANIMATOR #2. Trying my luck over in comic books. You in?

KIRBY. Comic what?

ANIMATOR #2. The new comic books — It's like they threw out the rest of the newspaper but the Funnies, and sell 'em directly to kids for a dime a pop. They've run out of the syndicated stuff, so now they're paying for original features.

KIRBY. How much?

ANIMATOR #2. Ten, eleven bucks a page.

KIRBY. (that's a fortune) Point me in the right direction!

They take off.

Fox Features Syndicate Bullpen, 42nd & Lex. 1940.

COMIC BOOK ARTISTS burst on stage, chewing gum, throwing paper balls at each other, smoking, cranking up the radio, which plays a New York Giants BASEBALL GAME. They sit at the disarranged drawing tables (which they leave disarranged).

ARTIST #1. Hey, I got three more pages to ink by noon! *WE NEED MORE COFFEE IN HERE!*

ARTIST #2. *(reaching for a cutout Sunday strip)* Let me see that clipping. I gotta swipe the punch in last Sunday's *Terry and the Pirates.*

ARTIST #1. You wait your turn. I'm swiping it! Somebody turn that radio to the Dodgers game, hanh?

ARTIST #2. Screw you and your Bums! The Giants are playing the Boston Braves at the Polo Grounds!

ARTIST #1. Dodgers!

ARTIST #2. Giants!

VICTOR FOX, a short, bald, excitable Wall Street type, enters, with JOE SIMON trailing. Everybody quickly shapes up.

FOX. *I'M THE KING OF THE COMICS, BOYS! KING OF THE COMICS!*

ARTIST #1. You're the King, Boss!

"Meet my Art Director, Jack Kurtzberg. He was at Fleischer, across town, before they had their labor troubles." (Photo: Hunter Canning)

FOX. Apparently we've been getting complaints about misspellings in our comic books, so I went out and got us an editor. He used to be a cartoonist at the Hearst papers in Syracuse, so watch your language. Boys, meet Joseph Simon!

SIMON. Hello. I'm sure it's gonna be a real pleasure working with you fellas.

FOX. *(to Simon)* You know, I once knew a whore in Syracuse. They said she was the best whore in town. I wasn't impressed! It's a small town.

SIMON. Uh...

Before Simon can articulate a response, Kirby enters with a stack of blank art boards, which he starts handing out to the artists.

FOX. Meet my Art Director, Jack Kurtzberg. He was at Fleischer, across town, before they had their labor troubles.

KIRBY. *(shakes Simon's hand)* "Art Director" means I'm the paste-up guy.

SIMON. How do you do.

Kirby goes back to what he was doing.

FOX. *(to Simon)* There better not be any labor troubles here, Sergeant — that's your job. I don't want no Rembrandts—Production, that's my watchword. This comic book thing? Trust me, it ain't gonna last. The kids are all going nuts over Superman now. All they want to see is costumed heroes beating up mad scientists, but I've seen trends come, and I've seen trends go, and this one'll be gone before the year is out. But before then we gotta separate as many dimes from little monsters as possible, because—

He points to the staff.

ARTISTS. *(Kirby too) THERE ARE MORE MORONS THAN PEOPLE!*

FOX. Atta boys! Carry on, Sergeant! *I'M KING OF THE COMICS!*

ARTIST #2. You're the king, Boss!

Exit Fox.

SIMON. Okay boys, what do we got? The third issue of *Mystery Men Comics*, the fifth issue of *Wonder World Comics*—

Fox returns.

FOX. Oh, yeah. I almost forgot, Sergeant. Not long ago I figured out a surefire formula for comic book success. Something every single Fox Features comic book story has to have.

SIMON. What's that?

FOX. On every story, put a big explosion on the third panel of the first page.

SIMON. *(beat)* What?

FOX. A big red and yellow explosion! *KPOW!* Third panel! First page! The kids eat it up like Pavlov's dog!

SIMON. But—

FOX. *RED AND YELLOW, SERGEANT!!* Or it's your job!

He leaves again. Kirby hands Simon a stack of boards.

KIRBY. I wouldn't worry about it, Joe. The boss is color blind.

SIMON. *(under his breath)* I gotta get outta here...

(to Kirby)

Jack, I hate to do this to you, but I can already see we're running short on this month's *Fantastic Comics*. I gotta assign you another eight-pager, due by the end of the week.

KIRBY. No problem. I'm not doing anything right now anyway.

SIMON. What about that "Blue Beetle" story Fox assigned you this morning?

KIRBY. I just handed it to you.

Simon looks through the art boards, incredulous.

SIMON. You...laid out and pencilled the whole thing?

KIRBY. Yeah.

SIMON. Before lunch?

KIRBY. Yeah.

SIMON. This looks great!

Kirby shrugs and grunts. He tries to walk away, but Simon grabs him by the arm, steering him into a corner.

SIMON. How much you making here?

KIRBY. Fifteen a week.

SIMON. Would you like to make eighty-five?

KIRBY. Would I!

SIMON. *(looks around conspiratorially)* Meet me in my apartment, tonight. Haddon Hall, uptown, near Columbia.

The artists clear out the drawing tables to make room for Simon's apartment. The radio, left behind, softly plays SWING MUSIC.

SIMON. We wanna increase our income, we gotta increase our output. Marty Goodman over at Timely Comics is paying fourteen, fifteen dollars a page for new comic book characters. Between your speed and my horse sense I figure we can triple the money Fox is paying us if we moonlight over there too.

KIRBY. *(taking out pages.)* I've got some sci-fi strips I wrote and drew on my on. Cosmic Carson. He's just like Elliot Ness.

SIMON. Elliot Ness never wore a fishbowl on his head that I was aware of.

KIRBY. You ever try busting gangsters on Saturn without one?

SIMON. That's cute, Jack, but we gotta go for something that'll sell.

KIRBY. It'll sell because it's good!

Simon LAUGHS at him.

KIRBY. What's so funny?

SIMON. I love you. Seriously, kid. Deeply and truly. How'd you fall into this racket again?

KIRBY. I was gonna jump off a roof if I turned into my dad.

SIMON. Tell me about it. My dad was a tailor.

KIRBY. Mine worked in a sweatshop.

SIMON. Pants!

KIRBY. Pants!

They toast.

KIRBY. Fucking pants.

Simon picks up the pages Kirby showed him.

SIMON. I like this. I do. And I get it, you like the *Amazing Stories* stuff, and that's great. But this isn't about what you want. This is about they want. The kids want Superman, we

36

gotta give them a Superman. Only different. An idea nobody's done before. Fox's got "Blue Beetle," right, so why not different animals, like a bird?

KIRBY. Hawkman. They got that at National.

SIMON. Cat?

KIRBY. Wildcat. National.

SIMON. Fish.

KIRBY. Sub-Mariner at Timely, Aquaman at National—

SIMON. Okay, forget animals. Elements. Fire—

KIRBY. The Human Torch. Timely.

SIMON. Earth—

KIRBY. Rockman. Also Timely.

SIMON. Air—

KIRBY. Airman. Centaur.

SIMON. Water! Hah!

Kirby looks at him.

SIMON. Aquaman, Sub-Mariner, right, right. Geez, this is harder than it looks...

They sit in silence for a time, thinking. The music on the radio is interrupted by a news bulletin:

RADIO ANNOUNCER. We interrupt this broadcast for an important news bulletin: Paris has fallen to the Third Reich. Nazi Panzers and Stormtroopers roll through the once-proud French capital as British forces retreat...

German Führer Adolf Hitler is now the undisputed master of the European continent.

The sound of HITLER addressing a cheering crowd comes out of the radio.

Simon and Kirby listen to it for a second, then Simon gets up and turns the radio OFF.

SIMON. Say ... maybe we're going about this the wrong way.

KIRBY. Yeah?

SIMON. Yeah.

(beat)

Maybe we should start with the villain.

"Maybe we start with the villain." (Photo: Crystal Skillman)

Timely Comics Bullpen, West 42nd St. 1941.

MARTIN GOODMAN, publisher of Timely, enters, holding art boards, Simon & Kirby following.

SIMON. So, Mr. Goodman, what do you think? A good fit for Timely Publications?

GOODMAN. You want your hero punching Adolf Hitler in the face on the cover of the first issue?

SIMON. He's Captain America! The superhero that represents patriotism! That smashes the US's enemies! It's what he does.

GOODMAN. But Hitler? A real person? On the cover? In the face?

(to Simon, sotto)

Can he sue us?

SIMON. The guy's dictator of Europe, Mr. Goodman, I don't think he's the litigious type.

KIRBY. Yeah, he'll just plow some tanks through the Bullpen!

Kirby laughs; Simon & Goodman glare at him.

GOODMAN. *Captain America Comics,* huh?

He hands the boards back to Simon.

All right. I'll need sixty-four pages of story by the fourth.
You two better know what you're doing.

He leaves.

SIMON. Sixty-four pages? By the fourth? We're going to have
to hire a couple more artists—

KIRBY. Aw, no! There's no way you're cutting down my page
rate. I got parents and a little brother to feed back on
Suffolk Street.

SIMON. But sixty-four pages? Even you're gonna have a tough
time—

KIRBY. Trust me.

*Kirby sits down at his drawing table as Simon leaves. While he
stares at the drawing board, a Ludlow Street Gang Member
saunters onto stage.*

LUDLOW #1. *(beat)* Christ-killer.

*Members of the Company rush on-stage and engage in a furious,
amorphous, tangled battle. Inspired, Kirby explodes into a fury of
drawing.*

KIRBY. I knew violence. I made it real. Give those Nazis what-
for, Cap!

*LIGHTS SHIFT. Goodman bursts out of his office. Scene flows
continuously even though two months have passed; Goodman
stands there. Everyone stops and stares at him. Beat.*

GOODMAN. One...million copies. I just got off the phone
with the distributor. The first issue of *Captain America
Comics* sold one million copies. We've blown "Superman"
and "Batman" out of the water!

*Everybody CHEERS and Kirby goes back to work after they clear
out.*

A teenage STANLEY LIEBER enters, climbs on a filing cabinet in the rear of the room, and starts playing a flute or a recorder off-key.

Kirby keeps working, trying to ignore Stanley, but finally he just turns and glares at him.

Simon enters with some scripts he's copy-editing.

KIRBY. *(to Simon)* What is that?

SIMON. That is Martin's cousin-in-law, Stanley. He made me hire the kid as an assistant. It's tough finding enough things to keep him occupied.

(to Stanley)

Hey, kid! You finish that prose story I assigned to you?

(to Kirby)

The Postal Service makes us put text pages in the comics so they qualify for Second Class mailing privileges.

Stanley hands Simon a few typewritten pieces of paper.

STANLEY. You bet! Here it is, Joe: "Captain America Foils the Traitor's Revenge!"

SIMON. *(looks at it)* Who's "Stan Lee?"

STANLEY. Me! That's my pen name! I'm gonna write the Great American Novel some day, so I gotta save my real name for that! I decided to change my name, just like Jack!

KIRBY. I changed my name to Kirby so it'd sound less Jewish, kid.

SIMON. Yeah, and you changed your name so it sounds Chinese. You traded one pissed-on minority for another, Stanley!

Kirby and Simon laugh. A tiny BELL rings offstage.

STANLEY. That's Martin! Time for his saltines and milk!

He leaves.

KIRBY. If he plays that damn flute while I'm trying to work one more time I'm gonna start throwing things at him.

SIMON. Simmer down, he's harmless.

The phone rings. Simon answers.

SIMON. Timely Comics, home of "Captain America," "United States Man" and "Mr. Liberty." Accept no imitations.

CRANK CALLER. You the editor of *Captain America Comics?*

SIMON. Yeah.

CRANK CALLER. I want you to look out your window and pick a lamppost on Times Square, you dirty Jew cocksucker, because when Hitler comes we're gonna hang you from it—

SIMON. Oh, you want the editor-in-*chief.* Here he comes now.

Stanley returns across stage; Simon grabs him, cupping a hand over the phone.

SIMON. Stanley, you're not going to believe this! One of your biggest fans is on the line. He read your last text page and he thought it was the cat's pajamas!

STANLEY. Well I'll be! Thanks, Joe!

Simon hands him the phone.

STANLEY. Hello?

Stanley, horrified by the invectives screamed at him, slams the phone down.

STANLEY. He called me all sortsa names! That's not funny, Joe!

SIMON. Then why am I laughing?

Exit Stanley. Simon pokes Kirby in his right arm, screwing up his drawing.

SIMON. Wanna grab lunch?

KIRBY. C'mon, what are you doing? I'm drawing here! That was a perfect Panzer!

SIMON. Sorry, sorry. You got to erase it?

KIRBY. *(beat)* Nah. It'll just slow me down. Next panel.

SIMON.*(looking around)* Is to be continued. You wanna go to lunch.

KIRBY. Nah, you go without me. I got twelve pages to tear through before I can come up for air. And I got all of "Captain America versus the Camera Fiend and His Darts of Doom" tonight.

Simon grabs Kirby by the arm and tries to haul him out of his chair.

SIMON. Sounds like way too much work to do on an empty stomach. Let's go!

KIRBY. What gives? I could drop you like a sack of manure!

SIMON. C'mon, I ever steer you wrong before?

Simon leads Kirby out onto the street.

KIRBY. What's the big idea?

SIMON. Don't be so thick! I couldn't say anything up there.

(produces a dime)

You know what this is?

KIRBY. A dime.

SIMON. You got some?

KIRBY. Sure. A couple.

SIMON. Just a couple, though.

KIRBY. Yeah, I could count 'em, if you—

SIMON. That won't be necessary. Unless you have about sixty
thousand, eight hundred and seventy-two of them.

KIRBY. What are you getting at?

SIMON. I've been talking to Goodman's accountant. For over
a year now I hear "Captain America" is doing great, I see it
flying off the newsstands. But "Overhead!" Goodman keeps
saying, "Overhead!" So no royalties for you and me. But at
dinner last night his own accountant shows me the books
—"Captain America" has been in the black since Day One!

KIRBY. He's a welsher.

SIMON. They're all pirates in this business, Jack, all pirates.
You should consider yourself lucky you have me looking
out for you. Now c'mon, let's go to lunch.

KIRBY. I lost my appetite.

SIMON. You'll get it back. See that tall building over there on
Lex?

KIRBY. That's an office building. There aren't any restaurants
in there.

SIMON. We're dining in today, Jack. In the office of National
Comics.

KIRBY. National Comics!

A HEAVENLY CHORALE blares.

A SEXY SECRETARY comes out to answer the phone.

SEXY SECRETARY. Good afternoon, National Comics, home of "Superman Comics," "Batman Comics" and "Wonder Woman Comics." Hold, please.

She holds her hand over the phone as JACK LIEBOWITZ, National's publisher, enters.

The chairman of Warner Brothers on line one.

LIEBOWITZ. Tell him to jump in a lake! I'm fraternizing with genius.

He shakes hands with Kirby.

Jack Kirby. A real honor. Your drawings leap off the page and punch you in the face! I love it!

SIMON. Joe Simon, Mr. Liebowitz. We spoke on the phone.

LIEBOWITZ. Right. You must be the business half of this duo. You own the suit. A pleasure. I'll level with you fellas. National's sick of competing with your Captain America, so we'd be more than happy to give you a year's contract to create new comics material for National for, say, $500 a week?

Kirby can hardly believe his ears, but Simon keeps it cool.

SIMON. And name billing on the covers of all books we do for you.

LIEBOWITZ. *(chuckles)* Artists and writers never get name billings on the covers, Mister ... Simon, was it? In comics it's the characters that are the stars. Superman, Batman. Never the artists.

SIMON. Take it or leave it.

LIEBOWITZ. *(beat)* I'll draw up the contracts. Have your lawyers give our legal people a call.

Exit Liebowitz.

Simon and Kirby return to the street, reveling in their triumph. Kirby interrupts:

KIRBY. We have lawyers?

SIMON. I'm dating a girl who has a cousin who knows a guy. Only thing is, we gotta come up with another hit series.

KIRBY. You kidding me? That's the fun part!

He sits at his desk, ready to work.

SIMON. I been thinking. You know how we gave Captain America that kid sidekick, Bucky, to give him somebody to talk to while he's kicking Nazi tail?

KIRBY. Sure. The little pest.

SIMON. Since the kids seem to relate to him so much, why don't we cut out the adult hero altogether?

KIRBY. Send out the kids to fight Hitler themselves. Yeah, I see it.

STANLEY. I think it's swell!

Stanley leaps out of his hiding place, scaring the crap out Simon & Kirby.

KIRBY. *JESUS CHRIST!!*

SIMON. Where'd you come from, Stanley?

STANLEY. C'mon, I could tell you guys were up to something secret! C'mon, you guys can use me! I can be like your sidekick! I can get you coffee, art supplies, milk, saltines—

KIRBY. We don't need any saltines!

(to Simon)

We don't need this kid, Joe.

SIMON. I don't know. It might be useful to have another pair of hands around. Look, Stanley, this is some real hush-hush, top secret stuff we got going on here. You can't tell your cousin Martin about it. Or any of the other eighteen hundred relatives he's got working for him.

STANLEY. Scout's honor, Joe! My lips are sealed!

He takes off.

KIRBY. You're gonna regret this.

SIMON. Give the kid a break. We can rent a hotel room near Timely and work on the National stuff during our lunch hour. Stanley can run us over stuff.

KIRBY. Let's get back to Timely. I still got the latest issue to get done and—

SIMON. Slow down, Jack! You're always rushing around! Listen, Doris has a friend she's trying to set up. You want to go to the movies with her and me tonight?

KIRBY. I was gonna work from home tonight.

SIMON. Jack ... you ever think—

KIRBY. What?

SIMON. You ever think you might try enjoying yourself a bit before then?

KIRBY. I'm going home. To work, Joe.

Kirby carries his portfolio home to find his young neighbor,
ROSALIND "ROZ" GOLDSTEIN, locked out of her apartment,
upset.

ROZ. Oh no. Oh no.

KIRBY. Hey Kid, you all right? I'm Jack. Jack Kirby. I live
upstairs.

ROZ. Rosalind — "Roz."

KIRBY. What's wrong, Roz?

ROZ. I can't find my key and they my whole family went out to
my stupid kid sister's concert and they locked the door —
and you said your name was Kirby? I thought the family
above us was the Kurtzbergs—

KIRBY. Kirby's my, y'know, pen name. I'm an artist.

ROZ. Oh, I bet your parents don't like that one bit.

KIRBY. Yeah my mother thinks it's worse than Hitler. But the
art with that name on it got us out of the East Side slums.
Out here, to glorious Brooklyn.

ROZ. *(laughs)* Oh. Yeah. The Promised Land. I've seen you out
there. Playing stickball.

KIRBY. Yeah?

ROZ. I remember thinking, "He looks like John Garfield but
he's so short!" I'm sorry. I like to talk.

KIRBY. So I see.

ROZ. Yeah. Blah blah blah! That's me. It drives everybody crazy.

KIRBY. It's fine by me.

ROZ. Yeah?

KIRBY. Yeah. So, Roz...

ROZ. Yeah?

KIRBY. You just gonna hang out here on the porch waiting all alone...?

ROZ. Or what?

KIRBY. I don't know - want to go upstairs, and ... see my etchings?

ROZ. Um ....

Kirby hands some comic book pages to Roz.

KIRBY. I have some here, but the stuff I'm working on now is up there.

ROZ. Oh!

KIRBY. What?

ROZ. Ah — you... You actually *have* etchings.

KIRBY. I told you, I'm an artist.

ROZ. Wow you sure are.

(going through pages)

With lots grown men in long underwear — beating each other up.

KIRBY. Yeah. Wanna come up? See some more drawings I mean.

ROZ. Maybe. Sure.

Simon returns as Roz leaves.

KIRBY. I gotta tell you.

SIMON. What?

KIRBY. I like enjoying myself. I like Roz. A lot.

Simon makes an "I told you so" gesture.

So, about our new hero—

SIMON. I'm thinking heroes. A kid from each Allied country. Holland, England, France, the US—

KIRBY. Yeah ... we could make the American a tough street kid from Brooklyn. Like "Dead End Kids." You got a title?

SIMON. I'm thinking on it —

They try to head off-stage but are stopped by the entrance of Goodman.

GOODMAN. So. Working for another company. Behind my back.

SIMON. Hi, Martin.

(beat)

I guess it's time for us to leave.

GOODMAN. You're fired!

(beat)

After you finish the tenth issue of "Captain America."

Goodman clears out.

KIRBY. Stanley. That little cocksucker...

SIMON. Jack—

KIRBY. He ratted us out the first chance he got!! *IF I EVER SEE THAT LITTLE PISHER AGAIN I'LL RIP HIS FUCKING HEAD OFF—*

SIMON. Jack, calm down! We don't know that! Everybody in this business knows everyone else. Besides, who cares? We get to work for National that much quicker.

KIRBY. For our new idea we have no title for?

SIMON. Well. As a kid I always liked that book *Boy Allies*... What do you think of *Boy Commandos*?

A CORPORAL steps out of the wings and hands Kirby a telegram. He reads it.

KIRBY. I think I'm gonna be one. This boy's gotta report to Basic Training in August.

SIMON. It'll be good for research.

Roz helps him put on his uniform. He takes out a ring. She gasps. He puts it on her finger.

ROZ. Yes, yes, yes, yes!

KIRBY. Well ... I guess I don't even have to ask the question. Say, honey you're taking all this really well.

ROZ. What?

KIRBY. I mean ... I'm going to war, baby.

ROZ. You are and you're going to come back.

KIRBY. You're sure about that?

ROZ. You're the hero.

KIRBY. Roz...

"Yes, yes, yes, yes!" (Photo: Hunter Canning.)

ROZ. You're my hero, honey. And I won't be lonely because you'll write me Jack! And draw - everything you see! Sheets and sheets. Every day you promise!

KIRBY. I'll try!

Behind them enters PATTON.

PATTON. She's right boy! Correspondence is a real art! Words! That's what they remember. Take a lesson from my letters son: Quote! I hope that in the final settlement of the war you insist that the Germans retain Lorraine, because I can imagine no greater burden than to be the owner of this nasty country where it rains every day and where the whole wealth of the people consists in assorted manure piles. End quote!

(beat)

P.S. Of course these remarks are intended for a joke. I label it because some of my jokes are not always appreciated. *NOW MOVE OUT MOTHERFUCKERS!*

Alsace-Lorraine, on the French/German border. 1944.

KIRBY. *(writing)* Dear Roz: General Patton drove Third Army like cattle across France after D-Day. But by the end of the summer — on the German border — we ran out of everything! Food! Water! Ammo! We were stuck where we were: Metz, the giant fortress-city, over the Moselle River.

Patton enters carrying a map and a pearl-handed pistol, furious.

PATTON. What are you fuckers doing here, huh? What are you fucking doing here? You fuckers are fucking up the whole thing! You're dead, you know that? You motherfuckers are supposed to be *FUCKING. DEAD.*

Patton confers heatedly (sotto) with Kirby's terrified C.O., a LIEUTENANT.

KIRBY. Someone must have radioed to Command our unit had been wiped out. It hadn't. But that screwed up the general's whole strategy. His beautifully laid-out battle plan. He didn't see us as people. Just a page being penciled. Move this here, that there.

(to audience)

George C. Scott? Him I'd follow to Hell and back. This cocksucker?

(grunts and shakes his head)

PATTON. I will fill that fucking jeep with your fucking dog-tags if you don't cross that fucking river!

He storms off. Kirby's lieutenant sits, weary.

"I will fill that fucking jeep with your fucking dog-tags if you don't cross that fucking river!" (Photo: Hunter Canning.)

KIRBY. Private Third Class Kirby, reporting for assignment, sir.

LIEUTENANT. *(Southern accent)* Private Third Class Kirby? Your name is Kirby, soldier?

KIRBY. That's right, sir.

LIEUTENANT. Not *Jack* Kirby, the cartoonist?

KIRBY. Yes, sir! I draw *Captain America*—

LIEUTENANT. And *Boy Commandos!* You're something else, you know that boy?

KIRBY. Yes, sir! I mean — thank you, sir!

LIEUTENANT. So you can draw.

KIRBY. Of course I can draw. I should be like Bill Maudlin, running around drawing cartoons of guys in jeeps, so the folks back home'll know what's going on over here—

LIEUTENANT. You're right, Private. No guard detail for you. I'm making you a scout. *(hands him a map)* Here. Go into these towns we don't control. See if you can find any Germans. Mark on these maps positions of tanks, mortar emplacements, camps. Come back here, give me a full report.

He exits, leaving Kirby standing there by himself.

KIRBY. Dear Roz, I have been made a scout. Somebody wants to kill you in the army, they make you a scout. The human target. I make my way through these old French towns, four, five, six hundred years old, like nothing we got in the States. This beautiful architecture, now just piles of rocks in the mud. The rain coming down. Always with the rain. It made your heart break, just the stupid, stupid cruelty of it. Once, I was walking through the middle of some ruined

57

village, and this mangy, starved dog came out of a hotel and he looked up at me with these eyes, these pathetic, shallow eyes..."How could you?" I went inside the hotel, to get out of the rain. It had these iron spiral staircases, velvet drapes, like something from the movies.

Kirby, inside the hotel, leans his rifle against the wall then bends over to tie his bootlaces.

A GERMAN SOLDIER hiding out in the hotel as well approaches from behind, rifle in hand.

GERMAN SOLDIER. Hey, Yankee. Fuck you.

Kirby freezes.

GERMAN SOLDIER. Get out, Yankee.

KIRBY. Nah — nah, you get out!

GERMAN SOLDIER. Fuck you! You get out!

KIRBY. No, you get out! This is the fucking Hotel Americain, now!

GERMAN SOLDIER. Hau' ab, du Hurensohn! Hau' ab![1]

KIRBY. What's that? "Hurensohn?" *WHORE*-son? You talking about my MOTHER? So sprecht ihr von meiner Mutter nicht! My parents came from Austria! *ICH BIN STERREICHER WIE DEINER FÜHRER, SCHWEIN!*[2]

---

[1] "Get out, you whoreson! Get out!"

[2] "You don't talk about my mother like that! ... *I'M AUSTRIAN, LIKE YOUR FÜHRER, PIG!*"

"Somebody wants to kill you in the army, they make you a scout." (Photo: Crystal Skillman)

Screaming wildly, Kirby dives for his rifle, making the German soldier flee. Kirby fires after him.

KIRBY. Never talk about a guy's mother! Never, you hear me! It's how we do things on the Lower East Side! *(To audience, exhausted:)* We called it "Butcher's Work," going through these abandoned towns nobody held because nobody wanted 'em, and mixing it up with whatever Germans we could find. This one dumb bastard, he got punched through a wall by a steel-jacketed bullet and his helmet flew off. I found some photographs in it. Him with his sweetheart, him with his parents when he was six, wearin' ... little fuckin' lederhosen. Dumb bastard. One minute you're playing in the street, the next minute— blooie. Some crazy comic book artist blows your fucking head off. Then I'd come back to base camp ... in this haze of murderous anger ... you'd come back, and...

A CORPORAL walks by, handing out mail. He hands a letter to Kirby.

CORPORAL. Mail call! Got one from your wife, Kirby.

Roz appears, writing frantically.

KIRBY. *(opens & reads)* "Dear Jack: How do I love you? Let me count the ways. I love you to the depth and breadth and height my soul can reach..."

ROZ. Yes! Oh yes!

KIRBY. "Let me not to the marriage of true minds/Admit... 'impediments.' Love is not love/Which alters when it alteration finds." *(beat)* Huh?

ROZ. Do you know how many love poems there are to copy from out of the Brooklyn Public Library?! We don't need all those King Arthur-y "thee's" and "thou's." We're from Brooklyn. "O, no! Love is the star to every wandering bark,/ Whose worth's unknown, although his height's been taken."

KIRBY. With each word, each letter ... after a while...

ROZ. "Love not alters with time's brief hours and weeks,/But bears it out..."

KIRBY. I'd feel myself turning back into a human again...

ROZ. "... even to the edge of doom."

KIRBY. After spending most of the day ... as a monster... the villain turned back to... Maybe not the hero. But close enough.

Patton returns.

PATTON. If commissioned officers did their full duty, then there would be no Trench Foot in Third Army. To win the war, we must not only conquer the Third Reich, but Trench Foot. All commanding officers must continuously remind the men of the importance of clean, dry socks. Only clean, dry socks can crush Hitler!

KIRBY. Clean socks or not, my legs turned purple and puffed up like an elephant's. I got sent to a hospital in Paris, then back to New York. I was one of the lucky ones. I saw some guys with black legs. Black legs fell off. First thing Roz said when I walked in:

ROZ. Oh, I hope your drawing hand's okay!

Jack kisses Roz.

The Kirby home. East Williston, Long Island. 1947. Kirby throws on a bathrobe, yawning. It's about noon.

KIRBY. She never pretended to understand the superheroes. But she was one in how she took care of me. Gave me a family.

ROZ. Kids!

KIRBY. Four! A whole studio of Kirbys!

ROZ. Kids! Get over here! You've got to get to school - no you don't get to stay at home and just ... draw funny pictures all day like daddy. I don't care what the other dads do — he is not unemployed — your dad is an artist!

KIRBY. Kids. They always know ... me and Joe were out of work. The Boy Commandos won their war. So their series got cancelled.

ROZ. No work today?

KIRBY. Nope. Not today.

(yawns)

I'm gonna "create" on the mural in the upstairs bathroom.

ROZ. You've been painting that mural for two weeks! Tropical fish are gonna cover the toilet!

Simon enters, carrying art boards.

"I don't care what the other dads do — he is not unemployed — your dad is an artist!" (Photo: Crystal Skillman)

SIMON. Rosalind, my girl! What's the good word?

ROZ. Hi, Joe. How's Harriet doing?

SIMON. Fine, fine. Expecting. Large and eating everything. Where's our boy? Mural?

ROZ. Mural.

SIMON. Well, let's put a stop to that right now...

ROZ. Jack!

Kirby returns. Simon hands him some art boards.

SIMON. Here's how I've been keeping myself busy. Take a look at this cover mock-up I drew.

ROZ. *(reading off board) Young Romance:* "I Was an Artist's Pick-Up. A 100% All-True Love Confessional. Designed for the more adult readers of comics."

KIRBY. *(deadpan)* "No, Linda — we can't go on like this! You know I'm engaged to your kid sister, Jane!"

ROZ. *(into it)* "But darling ... Jane is a child! She doesn't have the fire to kindle the spark of your genius! You need me, John!"

KIRBY. *(pointing to board)* And this is Jane, coming into the studio where no one can see her?

SIMON. *(as Jane, puts hand to her forehead)* "Oh, John..."

KIRBY. You gone queer or something?

SIMON. Queer for dollars! Lev Gleason's crime comics are flying off the stands! I've seen their market surveys. Over 50% of their readers are adults — guys our age.

KIRBY. What kind of a big revelation is that? In the Service, I
  got recognized all the time.

SIMON. Me, too.

KIRBY. How? You rode a horse up and down New Jersey for
  the Coast Guard the whole war!

SIMON. And during that time, how many successful U-boat
  attacks were launched against Atlantic City? Zero.
  (chuckles)
  You know what your problem is, Mr. Kurtzberg? You never
  learned how to play the system to your advantage. Losing
  Boy Commandos may be the best thing that ever happened
  to us. Time to focus on the adult market. They have more
  money to spend. Listen to me: next to True Crime
  magazines in the drug stores and the newsstands, what do
  you see?

KIRBY. Beats me. Prophylactics?

SIMON. Har, har. True Love magazines, ya dope! If Gleason's
  going for the guys, we'll go for the gals! What do you say?

KIRBY. *(shrugs)* Like I got anything else better to do.

SIMON. Great!
  Simon hands him a schedule, then exits. Kirby calls after him.

KIRBY. But this production schedule ... you better get me a
  few inkers on this Joe!

ROZ. I can do it.

KIRBY. Eh, this takes time to get right honey.

ROZ. Uh ... and why couldn't that be me again?

KIRBY. Cuz you've got a million things to do with the house and ...

Roz produces her own inked pages.

Holy smokes did you do this ....?

ROZ. Uh-huh. Like when you were showing me. Just stay in the lines, keep the shading and ... ohhhh ... that red-dressed diva is slapping her man right in the face for not listening to what the lady of his dreams can achieve!

KIRBY. *(playfully)* I work all night...

ROZ. So do I she said, with a tear in her eye.

KIRBY. Oh baby. You're good.

ROZ. Uh-huh!

They kiss.

Simon returns.

SIMON. Your art's perfect for the subject material, Jack. Idealized households, just like out of the Sears catalog! You make everything look like it's made out of Saran Wrap!

KIRBY. Yeah, Joe, "thanks." I was thinking...

SIMON. Yeah?

KIRBY. Maybe, now that we're successful, we got all these employees, and everything...

SIMON. Yeah?

KIRBY. I was wondering, maybe, I could write my own stories now?

SIMON. "Cosmic Carson" again, huh?

"Oh baby. You're good." (Photo: Hunter Canning)

KIRBY. More than that! I got "Starman Zero," and "Tiger 21," they're both strips about space — exploration of the stars! All this love stuff, it's so... mundane. Let's branch out!

SIMON. C'mon, mundane sells, Jack. Are you still on that science fiction kick? People think all those rockets and aliens are weird. They can't get into it.

KIRBY. So you say.

SIMON. Why are you busting my chops like this? You stick to the drawing table, it's your element. Your genius. Let me handle the rest. You remember what you said back at Fox, when I wanted our credits to read "by Simon & Kirby" instead of "by Kirby & Simon?"

KIRBY. Yeah, I said, "Whatever you say, Joe..."

SIMON. "...you own the suit." Right.

KIRBY. We both own suits now, Joe.

Joe considers a response. But then simply leaves. Jack exits in the opposite direction.

A GAVEL RAPS once, twice on the empty stage.

SCENE 8.

US Courthouse, Manhattan. April 21, 1954.

A table facing the audience, bearing a pitcher of water, a glass, and a microphone. We hear the sounds of COUGHING, PAPER SHUFFLING and so forth.

We hear the voice of Senator William Langer (R-ND), CHAIRMAN of the Senate Judiciary committee:

CHAIRMAN.*(Western accent)* The first witness this afternoon will be Dr. Fredric Wertham. Doctor, will you come forward and be sworn, please?

WERTHAM enters, stands behind the table, holds up his hand.

CHAIRMAN. Do you solemnly swear that the testimony you will give the United States Senate will be the truth, the whole truth, and nothing but the truth, so help you God?

WERTHAM.*(German accent)* I do.

CHAIRMAN. Doctor, do you have a prepared statement?

WERTHAM. Yes, a brief one.

CHAIRMAN. All right, Doctor, proceed in your own manner.

WERTHAM. Thank you.

(sits, reads from statement)

"I have practiced psychiatry and neurology since 1922. In 1929 I was the first psychiatrist to be awarded a fellowship by the National Research Council to do research on the brain. Some part of my research at that time was on brain syphilis. It came in good stead when I came to study comic books.

(drinks water)

"The question is this: are comics good? Or are they not good? If you want to raise a generation that is half Stormtrooper, and half cannon fodder, with just a dash of illiteracy, then comic books are good. In fact, they're perfect."

Kirby enters, observing.

WERTHAM. On the one hand, we have the Superman comic books. They arouse in children fantasies of sadistic joy in seeing people punished over and over again while you yourself remain immune. We have called it the Superman complex.

KIRBY. A couple of kids in leather jackets and duckbills knock over the local malt shop and Ozzie and Harriet think it's the end of Western Civilization. Middle America's looking for scapegoats, and this quack gives 'em comics! *COME ON DOWN TO THE LOWER EAST SIDE, I'LL SHOW YOU SOME JUVENILE FUCKIN' DELINQUENCY!*

WERTHAM. On the other hand, we have these so-called "romance" books.

KIRBY. But our love books aren't even for kids! It says so right on the cover! Look! "For the more adult readers of comics!"

*Wertham holds up **Young Romance.***

WERTHAM. On this one, here, we have the heading "For the more adult readers of comics," which seduces the young girl into thinking she's becoming part of something illicit, or sexual.

GASPS from the attendees. Simon enters and listens too.

KIRBY. Aw, gimme a break!

70

SIMON. It'll blow over, Jack.

KIRBY. He's calling us fascists!

SIMON. I know, Jack.

KIRBY. Me! A Jew who nearly got his ass shot off in France!

SIMON. Take it easy.

WERTHAM. Now, Mr. Chairman...I detest censorship. I
believe adults should be allowed to write for adults. I
believe that what is necessary for children is supervision. In
other words, if a father wants to go into a store and say, "I
have a little boy of seven. He doesn't know how to rape a
girl; he doesn't know how to rob a store. Please sell me one
of those comic books," by all means, let the clerk sell him
one! But I don't think the boy should be able to go see this
rape on the cover and buy the book. I thank you
gentlemen.

KIRBY. *(to audience)* Joe was right, like he always was. It did
blow over. Onto us.

*An INDUSTRY FLAK dashes on stage while the rest of the cast
clears away the Hearing set. She gestures like she's trying to quell a
riot.*

FLAK. Now, now. Though we of the comic book industry
wholly reject Dr. Wertham's outrageous accusations and
hysterical witch hunt, we of the newly-formed Association
of American Comic Magazine Publishers have voluntarily
chosen to adopt a Comics Code to guide the content of our
titles.

*She holds up the Comics Code document, with its famous seal large
on the cover.*

"Watch for the seal of the Comics Code Authority! And feel safe." (Photo: Crystal Skillman)

The forty-one provisions of the Comics Code constitute the most restrictive set of principles for any communications media in use today. Mothers of America! Remember! Watch for the seal of the Comics Code Authority! And feel safe.

The flak hands the Code document to Kirby as she leaves; he flips through it.

KIRBY. You were right, Joe, this could be a lot worse. This new Code thing doesn't affect us at all!

(sees Simon's distress)

What?

SIMON. It's over, Jack. Our company. Our partnership. It's all over.

KIRBY. No, no, no it's not! Listen to this: "The letters of the word 'Crime' on a comics cover shall never be appreciably greater in dimension than the other words in the title." We don't publish any books like that! Here's another: "No comics magazine shall use the words 'Horror' or 'Terror' in its title." See? We got nothing to worry about!

SIMON. You don't understand how this business works.

KIRBY. Hey! I been in it longer than you!

SIMON. Not the dirty part! The mud the magic stands on! I've tried to keep you from that. Listen:

(patiently)

The printer prints comics for us on credit. We sell the books to the distributors on credit, who sells them to the newsstands on credit.

KIRBY. Oh. Kay. So. What?

SIMON. Our distributor is Leader News Company.

73

He gets a blank look from Kirby.

What do you think they sell? "*Crime* Suspense Stories" and "Vault of *Horror*" and "Crypt of *Terror*!" All our credit was tied up with Leader! We can't pay our printer. They're bust, we're bust!

KIRBY. But ... but, maybe we could—

SIMON. No. We couldn't. I talked it over with my wife, and ... I'm getting out of the comics business for good. I got a job offer in advertising. I'm gonna take it.

KIRBY. But — what about Simon and Kirby? What about me?

SIMON. C'mon, Jack. We both knew this comic book thing was... temporary.

Exit Simon.

KIRBY. There was no work! No work, anywhere. Publishers were going bust left and right.

(beat)

I had to go back to the one place I swore I'd never go back to.

Stan Lee's office at Timely a.k.a. Marvel Comics, Empire State Building. 1961.

Kirby, holding his portfolio, approaches Stanley's isolated, cramped desk in the lonely corner of an office floor. Stanley is now 40 and known solely as STAN LEE.

KIRBY. Hey, Stanley. Remember me?

STAN LEE. Remember? How could I forget? Put 'er there, Tiger!

KIRBY. *(offers portfolio)* I brought some recent samples from the titles I've been penciling freelance. It's mostly from National. "Green Arrow," "Challengers of the Unknown," some sci-fi stuff—

STAN LEE. No, perish the thought! Put that portfolio away, that's for mortal creatures! Not you, Jack. Consider yourself hired! In the pantheon of comic art deities, you are the king! The Zeus! The Jupiter!

KIRBY. The Odin.

STAN LEE. Pardon?

KIRBY. King of the Viking gods. I've always been into Thor, Asgard, all that stuff.

STAN LEE. Huh! I'll have to remember that. Here, have a seat.

KIRBY. Boy, Martin's really got you squirreled away in the back room, here. I had to ask fifteen different guys from his other businesses how to get back here—

STAN LEE. Aw, I don't mind. It's been quiet, ever since that Senate hearing nuttiness. Like the whole fort ran for the hills the minute they saw Little Chief Red Bear and his braves coming over the ridge! Don't you worry though Jack! We'll hold the Injuns off together! Excelsior!

KIRBY. What?

STAN LEE. Hmm?

KIRBY. What is that?

STAN LEE. What is what?

KIRBY. "Excelsior."

STAN LEE. It's the motto of New York State.

KIRBY. Yeah? What's it mean?

STAN LEE. You know, I have no idea! I just started saying it one day. It's got this crazy ring to it! "Excelsior" *"Excelsior!"*

He lets it resonate—then, abruptly:

I'm the last man standing since Martin — and Doctor Wertham — cleared out the Bullpen. I've held this job since I was seventeen years old. Except for when I went into the Service.

KIRBY. You don't say.

STAN LEE. And Martin's run it pretty much the same way this whole time.

A flashback begins. Enter Goodman.

76

GOODMAN. The war is over, Stanley. The superheroes are dead! Kids are sick of fighting! They want to laugh — laugh! We need comedy! Funny animals!

He leaves.

STAN LEE. Stan the Man's all over it like a cheap suit, Boss!

(picks up phone)

Editorial? Here are our new titles: *Comic Capers, Comic Cartoons*—Wait! *Comic **Comics**!*

Goodman returns.

GOODMAN. There's a war on, Stanley! Why are you publishing all this phony-baloney funny animal crap! We're kicking Commie keister in Korea, and we've got to get the children of America behind the fight against International Oriental Bolshevism!

He leaves.

STAN LEE. Your wish is my command, O Publishing Aladdin!

(into phone)

Scratch our whole comedy line! Now it's *Battlefront! War Action! Battle Action! Battle War!* ***War Battle Action War!***

Goodman returns.

GOODMAN. Dear God, Stanley! Why do you have dead Asians all over my covers? It's 1956, for Christ's sake! We're not Klansmen! Have you seen the killing the Japs are making with these "Godzilla" movies? Science fiction! Horrors spawned by the atom bomb, Stanley, that's what kids want to see!

He leaves.

STAN LEE. Aye-aye, Cap'n!

(losing enthusiasm; into phone)

Yeah, okay, now we're gonna go with: *Tales to Astonish, Tales of Suspense, Strange Tales.*

(pulls comics out of desk, hands to Kirby)

Our latest four-color "masterpieces."

KIRBY. *(flips through comic)* "Groot, the Monster from Planet X." "I Was Captured by the Creature from Krogarr."

STAN LEE. Krogarrrrrr.

KIRBY. Hanh?

STAN LEE. You gotta trill your R's, like this: "The Creature from Krogarrrrr."

KIRBY. Krogarrrrr.

STAN LEE. Ain't it a scream? I spend half the day dreaming up these nutty titles —and they actually pay me for it! So. Thus you have seen the meagre spoils of my modest fiefdom, Sir Jack of Kirby, but what I have here at Marvel Comics is yours. Marvel— that's what we re-named Timely, after you and Joe left...

KIRBY. Yeah...

STAN LEE. Say why did you guys leave, anyway? I wasn't around to see it.

He looks at Kirby. Whether it's an honest question or a test, Kirby can't tell. Either way, it inspires an awkward pause.

KIRBY. *(chuckles)* Who can remember? That was a long time ago, Stanley—

STAN LEE. *(bristles)* Stan! Just Stan is fine. I actually had my name legally changed to Stan Lee.

KIRBY. Okay. I did the same with Kirby.

STAN LEE. Look at us. A couple of old phonies. Kurtzberg and Lieber. Showmen! And you know what? The show must go on. The pay is nothing fancy—

KIRBY. How not fancy?

STAN LEE. *(beat)* Thirty dollars a page.

KIRBY. Oy...

STAN LEE. I'd give my artists the shirt off my back if I could. And if they wouldn't think I was coming onto them. Marvel publishes eight titles a month, four stories an issue, a twelve page lead, six or eight pagers for the rest. I can give you as many as you want to tackle to start—

KIRBY. I'll do all of them.

STAN LEE. Come again?

KIRBY. All of them. I'll do all the stories in all of your books.

STAN LEE. That's twenty-eight stories — over three hundred pages a month, Tiger.

KIRBY. I need the work. And you know I can do it.

STAN LEE. *(beat)* I'll need to send some stories out to other artists— Ditko, Heck, Ayers— if only for variety's sake—

KIRBY. I got no problem with that. I'm your new one-man Bullpen.

STAN LEE. You know what you are, Tiger? You're the King! You're the King of the Comics!

KIRBY. Thanks, Stanle—

STAN LEE. Stan.

KIRBY. Stan.

Exit Kirby.

Goodman enters, wielding a gold club, startling Stan.

GOODMAN. You know who I've just been golfing with, Stanley?

STAN LEE. *What?* What now, Martin?

GOODMAN. Ask.

STAN LEE. Why, who have you been golfing with, Martin?

GOODMAN. Jack Liebowitz, over at National! He says their best selling title of 1961 is something called *Justice League of America.* Looks like the Long Underwear Men are back in a big way. So why the hell are you wasting my money with this juvenile monster junk! Superheroes, Stan! We need superheroes!

He leaves.

STAN LEE. I give up!

Kirby re-enters with portfolio.

KIRBY. Alright Stan, I've got "Gigantus" and "X, the Thing That Lived" for you...

STAN LEE. I quit!

KIRBY. What...?

STAN LEE. This — this stupid, boring, meaningless job was only supposed to be temporary, you know? But it's gobbled up two decades of my life! I've bent over backwards to please Martin, but this? Superheroes? Again? It's too much. I shall march into the publisher's office and hand in my resplendent resignation then sally forth to a land where writers are truly respected! Hollywood!

KIRBY. Whoa, whoa, whoa— Stan! I know it's your life and all, but I got four kids to feed! Who's gonna give me assignments if—

Stan stops him by putting his hand over his mouth.

STAN LEE. Your regal words would stay my hand any other time, O Comics King. But my course — nay, my destiny — is clear.

Chuckling, he starts to exit. Then turns suddenly. Beat.

You know, my wife says I should do the super hero title. But do something I might like to read. Something different, fresher.

KIRBY. Hey, yeah, that's not a bad idea, why don't you do—

Stan swiftly produces a two page outline and shoves it under Jack's nose. Clearly he's been holding on to it this whole time, awaiting the most dramatic moment to spring it.

STAN LEE. Here, I jotted some thoughts down.

KIRBY. *(reading)* "The Fantastic Four." You never get tired of alliteration, do you?

STAN LEE. It is mankind's most astonishingly awesome achievement.

KIRBY. *(scanning pages)* This is ... kinda thin. A page and a half? Just an outline. It's gonna need some fleshing out before it's a proper story.

STAN LEE. That's what I have you for.

KIRBY. *(touched)* You'd ... let me change stuff, Stan? Add to the story? I've always wanted to do more science fiction stuff.

Spaceships to the stars, alien civilizations, that kind of thing.

STAN LEE. Do whatever you want, as far as I care. As long as you, you know, stay in those guidelines. Why not? Who did Captain America? Boy Commandos? Young Romance, for cryin' out loud! You're what's known as bankable, Jackie Baby!

Kirby goes to his drawing table, prepares to work.

KIRBY. That's true! What've you done? Copy other publishers your whole career!

STAN LEE. Uh... Well, that's one way of putting it, I guess. Martin calls it "Adapting to current market trends"...

KIRBY. You gotta make the trends, Stanley, not follow 'em! Throw the first punch. I've known that since I was ten years old.

STAN LEE. Together, our combined creative catalysts will shake the halls of comicdom asunder. Who would dare stand in our way? Face Front, True Believers! Verily, I doth proclaim the Magnificent Marvel Age of Comics is about to begin!

KIRBY. *(beat)* Why can't you talk normal?

Blackout.

"Who would dare stand in our way?" (Photo: Hunter Canning)

Marvel Comics' offices. 1969.

LIGHTS UP on a cutting-edge Tom Wolfe-era NEW JOURNALIST.

NEW JOURNALIST. Anyone with their ear to the nation's quads knows that Stan Lee's *Fantastic Four* and other Marvel Comics are the hottest thing to hit campus since the bongo drums. What is the secret of his success? From Southern Illinois University:

Journalist interviews guitar-strumming folk rock STUDENT.

STUDENT #1. I saw my sister wearing a Spider-Man t-shirt and that's how I got my first Marvel Comic. My favorite is the Hulk, he's the innocent being hounded by the Man. Also, he's really good at kicking the army's ass.

NEW JOURNALIST. From Cornell:

She interviews a beatnik intellectual STUDENT.

STUDENT #2. The psychedelic cosmic-scapes of *Fantastic Four* and *Thor* display a depth of psychological examination and philosophical metaphor that make the reader ask deep, deep questions of the universe like "What is Human? What is the Divine? Do our thoughts and desires matter in the full panoply of space/time? And are you holding?"

(directly to New Journalist)

Seriously, are you?

Student 1 indicates he is in fact, holding. Thrilled, he and Student 2 go off together.

NEW JOURNALIST. How does "Stan the Man," as he's dubbed himself in the credits and letter columns of his own comics, do it?

LIGHTS UP on Stan Lee's office. He and Kirby appear to be in the middle of a "Fantastic Four" plotting session. The Journalist joins them.

NEW JOURNALIST. Here Stan Lee is in action at his weekly Friday morning plotting session with Jack "King" Kirby, a veteran comic book artist, a man who created many of the visions of your childhood and mine: The King is a middle-aged man with baggy eyes and a baggy Robert Hall-ish suit. He is sucking a huge green cigar and if you stood next to him on the subway you would peg him for the assistant foreman in a girdle factory.

STAN LEE. We've had the Fantastic Four fight Dragon Man — the Inhumans — but for our next ish I know we can go even bigger!

KIRBY. Ummh.

STAN LEE. This time — what if the whole ever-lovin' world is threatened? By a huge, god-like figure — Universus, Cosmicus ... Galactus!

He begins to pace up and down, gesturing dramatically and acting out the story.

KIRBY. I see.

STAN LEE. He comes to Earth to devour it — he feeds on the very energy of planets! And with him is a herald — the Silver Surfer — and he engages the FF in cataclysmic combat! He's too much, even for them! The FF lies defeated! Earth is on the brink of oblivion! Sue, Ben, Johnny, Reed ... they've failed humanity when humanity needed them most!

KIRBY. Right.

STAN LEE. Then!!! *SUDDENLY!!!!*

He looks at Kirby, who waves him along.

STAN LEE. The Silver Surfer has a change of heart — the nobility and bravery of the Fantastic Four makes him realize Earth is worth saving! He turns on his master! And though Galactus is beaten back, he uses his Power Cosmic to trap the Silver Surfer on Earth — where only the FF knows of his sacrifice. He's forced to wander the planet — forever — hated by the very people he gave everything up to save.

NEW JOURNALIST. Lee sags back on his desk, limp and spent! Kirby has leaped out of the chair he was crumpled in.

KIRBY. *(no enthusiasm)* Great, great.

NEW JOURNALIST. The cigar is out of his mouth and his baggy eyes are aglow. His high voice is young with enthusiasm. Stan Lee has done it again!

KIRBY. *(to journalist)* Cut the crap, huh?

NEW JOURNALIST. What?

KIRBY. That's not how Stanley and I "work together." This is what really happens:

The phone rings. Kirby answers.

KIRBY. Yeah?

STAN LEE. In the next issue, let's have the Fantastic Four fight God! 'Nuff said! Face front, Tiger! You're the *KING!*

He hangs up.

KIRBY. *(to New Journalist)* And now I gotta come up with twenty-four comics pages of story! And he gets all the credit, just because he writes out the dialogue after I turn the pages in! Which is based on my notes, written on the boards — a lot of which he ignores, thank you very much!

Kirby, demonstrating his own version of the past, shows boards to Stan.

STAN LEE. *(pointing)* Who's the shiny guy?

KIRBY. You told me to have 'em fight a god, right? Well God, who we're calling "Galactus," runs around the galaxy eating planets. He needs their energy to survive. So he needs somebody to go out and scout out the planets for him.

STAN LEE. *(squinting)* Is he on a...flying surfboard?

KIRBY. Yeah. He's the Silver Surfer. The herald of Galactus.

STAN LEE. What will you think of next? That's why they call you the King, Jack! King Kirby!

KIRBY. You call me that, Stan.

STAN LEE. And now all the hoary hosts of Marveldom do, too!

KIRBY. *(to New Journalist)* You gonna print that?

NEW JOURNALIST. Ehh. I like my version better.

KIRBY. Unbelievable.

New Journalist leaves. Stan goes back to work. Simon enters.

SIMON. He's got the suit, Jackie boy.

KIRBY. Hey, Joe. How's the advertising game treating you?

SIMON. It's better than being torn apart by hungry wolves. Some days.

KIRBY. The college kids are calling him a "modern-day Homer!" He gave a lecture at Carnegie Hall, for Christ's sake! *CARNEGIE HALL!! I MEAN WHAT THE FUCK?!*

SIMON. He brings the magic.

KIRBY. No, he doesn't. Sitting here, at the drawing table, working into the wee hours of the night, taking his three sentences and turning them into this — an actual comic, a story, something someone can lose themselves in — *that* is the magic.

SIMON. No, that's work.

KIRBY. *WORK IS MAGIC!!* Why doesn't anyone understand that? Why does everyone worship the bosses? That crazy butcher Patton they turn into a hero! And Stanley— you know who came by the offices the other day? Fellini! Fucking Fellini!

Famed film director FEDERICO FELLINI enters in a cloud of cigarette smoke.

FELLINI. I like very much your comics!

He walks right past Kirby and embraces Stan.

FELLINI. You are not so different you and I, you know? Movie director and the comic man?

He works Kirby's arms like a puppet's.

FELLINI. You work-a the artist's hands like the Father in Heaven fills the lifeless, disgusting lump of clay with life! You come to Rome! We make-a the movies together! You a modern-day Virgil, Signor Lee!

He leaves with Stan.

KIRBY. Virgil? Seriously?! *YOU'RE STILL PLAYING YOUR GODDAMN FLUTE, STANLEY!!*

SIMON. Why don't you call him out on it?

KIRBY. What?

SIMON. You see him every day. Why not ask for more credit. You're owed "co-plotter," at least.

KIRBY. I got a family, Joe. I got mouths to feed. I can't get a rep for being difficult—

SIMON. Jesus! Always with the family! Like you're the only one in the world who has one! That was your excuse for not leaving Fox. Remember? "I'm the King of the Comics, Sergeant!"

(laughs)

It kills me they call you that now.

KIRBY. King of the Comics. Great. World's Smartest Cockroach.

SIMON. Look. Kid. Reason I asked you to lunch today is... I'm gonna be doing a thing.

KIRBY. A thing?

SIMON. You know what copyright termination is?

KIRBY. For the sake of argument let's say that I don't.

SIMON. Law says, certain amount of time passes, twenty-eight years, after you sell a property to somebody, you can get the rights back.

KIRBY. Okay. So?

SIMON. Calendar says it's 1969. So, minus twenty-eight...

KIRBY. 1941... Holy shit, Joe, you're grabbing Captain America back?

SIMON. My lawyers already filed the papers.

KIRBY. Goodman's gonna go nuts! I'm gonna lose my job!

SIMON. I don't believe you. This is more than just this week's
rent, this is security for life! You know how much money
they're gonna pay me to keep hold of the Cap property?

KIRBY. This is gonna look bad, Joe. This is gonna look really
bad on me—

SIMON. I was hoping maybe you'd throw in with me, but—
You know what I don't understand, Jack? You draw people
punching each other in the face every day. You grew up in a
street gang, you served in fucking France. Yet you refuse to
stand up for yourself! You refuse to fight—

Kirby gets in his face.

KIRBY. You ever see the look on a guy's face when he realizes
both his arms been blown off by a land mine? No, because
you spent the war riding a horse for the Coast Guard,
which, incidentally, makes no god damn sense at all. You
ever see what a ten year old kid looks like after he gets
pushed off a five-story tenement roof during a block fight?
It's okay, I'll tell you Joe, because you grew up sipping tea in
Syracuse. The kid looks like a garbage bag filled with blood
and shit exploded.

(pokes a finger in his chest)

You fight. Hanh? I got my fill a long time ago.

*Kirby turns his back on Joe, heads toward the other side of the
stage, where Goodman and Stan Lee wait.*

SIMON. You can't hide in your art boards, Jack! The world will
find you! It always does.

*Fed up, Simon exits. Kirby and Goodman and Stan look at each
other.*

KIRBY. So.

GOODMAN. So.

KIRBY. Joe gonna get Cap back?

GOODMAN. I'm afraid I can't comment on on-going
negotiations.

KIRBY. You're probably just gonna pay him off, right? I know
Joe. He doesn't have a burning desire to regale the children
of America with the patriotic adventures of the Star-
Spangled Avenger. He wants a check.

GOODMAN. And what do you want, Jack?

KIRBY. What do you got?

GOODMAN. For my enemies? A wingtip up the ass. For my
friends? Well...

KIRBY. I want what he was gonna get.

GOODMAN. Come again?

KIRBY. Whatever you're paying Joe to keep Cap. That's what I
want.

GOODMAN. You'll sign a statement affirming our ownership
of the character—

KIRBY. Sure.

GOODMAN. That we always owned it, from the beginning—

KIRBY. You got it.

GOODMAN. And we own all the other characters you've ever
worked on, or ever created, while working here.

KIRBY. Including the ones... I did with Stanley?

GOODMAN. Especially them.

Kirby considers this.

Goodman produces a long check notebook, signs a check, tears it off to hand it to Stan, who hands it to Kirby.

GOODMAN. I'll have our lawyers deliver the papers to your house by courier tomorrow.

KIRBY. *(looks at check, whistles)* Joe always had the business sense.
GOODMAN. Anything else?

KIRBY. Yeah.

He tucks the check safely away.

KIRBY. I quit.

GOODMAN. What?

KIRBY. You wanna know why I signed that away so quickly? Huh? No, you wouldn't. All you know is how to read last month's sales sheet. Any idiot can do that. I can create. I can give up Cap, I can give up the Hulk, the X-Men, anything I made here— Because I'm just gonna make more. I can. This whole time I was here, I was making up my own line of characters.

(points to Stan)

That he can't take any credit for. And I'm taking them to National.

GOODMAN. You defecting again? The balls you got—

KIRBY. I been talking to them for a while. They're gonna let me write and draw — I'm doing the whole thing! At last!

STAN LEE. Jack, c'mon—

KIRBY. We'll see who the real fucking Homer is!

   He storms off.

San Diego Comic-Con. July 1982.

*A FAN accosts a visibly older Kirby as he crosses the Convention
Hall, carrying a comic book. Kirby signs it for him.*

KIRBY. There you go kid.

FAN. Wow. Wow. Kirby. Jack Kirby. *KIRBY!*

KIRBY. That's me.

FAN. I've been following your work with Stan like .... forever!
The minute I hear there was a con in my hometown — like
FINALLY — I mean we're so lucky you moved out near
San Diego. You doing stuff with the movies?

KIRBY. My kid has asthma actually. Warmer climate.

FAN. Oh! Did you read Stan's new interview in *Comics Now* —
all the movie stuff he wants to do with Marvel. Can you
imagine. All your guys on the big screen. Like maybe Thor!

KIRBY. Yeah, you like Thor, huh?

FAN. Are you kidding? Grew up on it, and now I'm reading it
to my kids.

KIRBY. What about the stuff I did on my own? *New Gods?*

FAN. *New Gods.* Ah... I tried, but it was a little too — cosmic
for me, you know? And who was your writer again?

KIRBY. Uh...

FAN. All those exclamation points! So over the top. Like somebody spitting on you while you talk. But movies you know. It's a good interview you should read it. It's insane. Look at me, going on and on like a goon. I should get into comics huh?

KIRBY. Yeah.

FAN. Man. Can I take a picture?

Before Kirby can give permission, the picture is taken — FLASH!

Excelsior!

He's about to leave, when he produces an original page/art board:

FAN. Oh! How could I forget — can you sign this too? The tour de force! An original — I think it's from *Fantastic Four,* what, post-Galactus, right? Like #67, #68?

KIRBY. Where did you get this? It *is* original...

FAN. Should be. I paid like half my savings. A thousand bucks.

KIRBY. A thousand bucks?

FAN. Yeah, like I can afford to give you any more of my money!

Fan leaves. Kirby returns to his hotel room.

Roz enters, taking notes on a spiral pad.

ROZ. I found eight more on the con floor! I wrote them all down! Names and addresses of art dealers selling stolen pages. *Your* pages.

KIRBY. I know.

ROZ. Crooks every one of them! These art dealers are robbing you blind! Where did they get these pages from? *Fantastic Four, Thor, Captain America, Iron Man. Avengers*— These are supposed to be your fans, but they're parasites! Where did they get this art in the first place?

KIRBY. From the offices, I guess. I heard the suits just gave them away as freebies to executives the company did business with — guys who made TV shows and toys and stuff. *(produces contract)* But if I sign this...

ROZ. What is that?

KIRBY. The lawyers mailed me this stupid form. I saw it first. I didn't want you to get mad, you always get mad—

ROZ. Why? What does it mean?

KIRBY. I sign it...

ROZ. And...?

KIRBY. They give me what they've got left.

ROZ. What's that?

KIRBY. Eighty-eight pages.

ROZ. Eighty-eight! Outta how many thousands?

KIRBY. I lost track. As many as it took to tell the stories I wanted to tell.

ROZ. Don't do it, Jack! The pages are bad enough, but they want you to sign away your rights — your art's on frisbees, movies — everywhere I look it's you, Jack. And you're not even there.

"These are supposed to be your fans, but they're parasites!"
(Photo: Crystal Skillman)

KIRBY. No one cares about anything new I do - all they want is the old stuff. Nothing new sells!

ROZ. But you can't let them just take away all the work you—

KIRBY. What choice do I have?

ROZ. Jack.

KIRBY. ...

ROZ. Do you know why I let you talk me into going up to your apartment that day we met? Because every day I'd hear you rushing up those stairs. Full of places to go, and I'd imagine you were coming to talk to me. Every girl growing up there trying to flirt you with you - all because they just wanted to get married — get out of there. You didn't care about them. And I loved you even more for it because what I loved is how you were always moving. Never sitting still. You get an idea and the room lights up and we talk for hours and I see... I see you. Without that, I don't know who I'd be ... who are our kids would be. What you've done, these heroes,, fighting, flying, running ... they're all you. If that isn't worth fighting for ... I don't what is. Because I've fought for it.

KIRBY .*(beat)* I'm not your hero, Roz. Every time I go in rooms with bosses and lawyers, I come out someone else.

Roz grabs his hand.

ROZ. Every single drawing that's come from this hand — you created. You've made up. From nothing and that's something - that's something Jack. You've got to find a way to come to peace with that...

She kisses his hand. He kisses her.

KIRBY. Let's get some sleep huh?

Roz exits. LIGHTS SHIFT as Kirby's dream begins. He enters an office and a chair is faced away from him.

KIRBY. Hello, Martin.

The chair swings around, revealing:

STAN LEE. Just me Jack. Crazy huh?! *PLOT TWIST!*

KIRBY. It doesn't matter who it is. You're all the same to me.

STAN LEE. Ah see, making me the suit. Well I like wearing suits. They're comfy.

KIRBY. Just cut to the chase Stan.

STAN LEE. That was always your problem, want to get right into the action! Throw the first punch before we even establish the situation. Make it clear we're old friends.

KIRBY. We weren't friends Stan.

STAN LEE. Now that hurts my feelings. And you know how sensitive I am. Look, I take the time to come out here, talk to you. I don't leave you to some flunky lawyer.

KIRBY. Why? What the hell do you guys want now?

STAN LEE. Look all this talk about who created who — taking characters back, sharing credit. That's not what it's really about is it?

KIRBY. It's the truth!

STAN LEE. Really? You're a big fan of the truth? Is your name really Kirby? I mean, come on. You were ashamed—

KIRBY. I was not! You take that back!

STAN LEE. What then?

"It doesn't matter who it is." (Photo: Hunter Canning)

KIRBY. I was never ashamed of being Jewish. But — Kirby.
You know, it sounded Irish. Tough. Nobody thought of
Jews being tough. If they grew up where I did, they'd know
better, but—

STAN LEE. So you consciously changed something you knew
wasn't true in order to get a better story, right?

KIRBY. You're twisting it all around! Who I am, what I did, I
was in those pages - it wasn't you telling me what to do. It
was me creating and you could have - you could have told
them, Stan.

STAN LEE. What's my sin? When people said I was a genius, I
said "Who, me?" And that made 'em only yell it louder! Li'l
ol' me!

(reverently)

Excelsior.

KIRBY. Those were my stories too!

STAN LEE. Let's say, just for the sake of argument, because I'm
a reasonable person, that you're right. Nobody cares, really,
whose stories they were. I love rocket ships and skyscrapers
falling over as much as the next guy, but in the end, you
focused on the wrong story, Jack. People want magic. Not
because they're innocent little children at heart but
because the world is a whirlwind of crazy and magic is a
simple way to make sense of it all. A genius—me—dictates
his ideas to talented craftspeople—you—and the result is
love and riches.

KIRBY. No. No. The work is the magic.

STAN LEE. If it was magic, it wouldn't be work, Jack! It is so
much easier to be something than it is to do something.

And that is why, no matter how many times this story is told, I will be the hero. You? The trusty sidekick!

JACK. I hate sidekicks.

STAN LEE. *(handing him release form)* You sign this, you get your art. And no more letters bothering us ok Jack, no more talking about who did this or who did that in interviews or conventions. Just ... you've done it before.

KIRBY. This says I give up royalties and future payments.

STAN LEE. If you sign we got a gift for you.

KIRBY. Eighty-eight pages. Do you know how many pages I've ... No money for reprints, no toys, no coloring books, no lunch boxes, and certainly, no fucking movies. The art boards, the physical art, I can sell them to the few people who actually know what my name is. I got four kids and a wife and nothing to give them when I'm gone.

STAN LEE. You know I've worked my whole life just like you - but every time you look at me I see it - disgust. For the new kid. Me. You always hated me, I get it. So just sign it, huh?

Kirby rips up contract. He turns to go.

STAN LEE. Oh man, nice scene, dramatic! Maybe you can write. But tomorrow when you've woken up - in reality - you sign. That's the truth, weeks later, when they come back with a counter, you sign. *You sign.*

He reaches into his suit jacket and produces a contract identical to the one Kirby ripped up. He shows Jack his own signature.

And you get the art. None of the good stuff, of course. That's long gone. Swear to God I wasn't even around when it vanished. But credit, you know that's just not ... I read ... I followed all you did after you left Jack. What you wrote on your own. It was good, that's the truth. Every interview

I've ever given, any article, any book I say you were the king, Jack - that you're the king of the comics - you know that's true.

KIRBY. You left me a nickname. You sure are a generous guy, Stan.

STAN LEE. At the end of the day, it's about what's right for the story, you know?

KIRBY. I've got to live mine.

STAN LEE. Everybody does. That's why you've gotta make shit up. Face Front, True Believer!

Sound of an auctioneer hammer coming down. Stan leaves.

Kirby is left alone on stage.

Sotheby's, 1994. Again.

The AUCTIONEER enters. She resumes the bidding of Kirby's artwork, continuing from the start of the play.

AUCTIONEER. Our next item. Original, pin-up of superhero Invisible Girl, from comics magazine *Fantastic Four* #10. Pencils by Jack Kirby. Bidding will also begin at five thousand dollars.

KIRBY. I'd just bring the art in, dump it off, collect my check and go home! I'd forget about the stuff! How was I supposed to know?

ACTOR PLAYING JOE. For many people, getting a piece of one's childhood is priceless. And that's what he is, it seems. A piece of everyone's childhood.

AUCTIONEER. Do I hear six thousand five hundred?

ACTOR PLAYING GOODMAN. How...many pieces of art are we discussing here?

AUCTIONEER. *SOLD!* To the gentleman in the rear for seven thousand, four hundred and seventy five dollars.

KIRBY. I worked for Martin from 1957 to 1969...

AUCTIONEER. Next: reproduction, cover, *Amazing Spider-Man #1.* Pencils by Jack Kirby.

KIRBY....on at least...forty titles...

AUCTIONEER. Bidding will begin at ten thousand dollars.

KIRBY. ...so it's gotta be in the neighborhood of ... twenty thousand pages. All sold to line some faceless guy's pockets.

AUCTIONEER. *SOLD!* To the man in the plaid, for fourteen thousand, nine hundred and fifty dollars!

She leaves, leaving Kirby alone. Beat.

KIRBY. Comics. They were supposed to be temporary.

A second FAN arrives as the Auctioneer exits.

FAN #2. *(gasping for breath)* Here...Mister Kirby...would you mind...signing this?

KIRBY. Sure. Slow down, you'll live longer.

(takes comic; puts on glasses)

"The Coming of Galactus!"

FAN #2. First appearance of the Silver Surfer!

KIRBY. Yeah...that was a good one.

FAN #2. It's the first thing I ever remember reading on my own. By myself. With my own two eyes.

(shakes his hand)

It's been really great meeting you, Mr. Kirby.

KIRBY. What's the rush? You just got here.

FAN #2. I'd love to stay, but I just drove ten hours from Chicago and I have to get back because I couldn't get the time off from work.

KIRBY. You drove ten hours from Chicago just to come here for fifteen minutes?

"After all ... you're the King." (Photo: Crystal Skillman)

FAN #2. Well...yeah! I figured this might be the only time I get to meet you. After all...you're the King.

Fan exits.

Beat.

Kirby goes to his desk. He lifts his pen. He can't do it.

KIRBY. Comics. They'll break your heart.

Kirby steps away from the desk. He takes out from his pocket that piece of chalk he once drew with as a kid.

He starts drawing on the floor of the theater — a hand, an arm, a body, a face — as he shares his idea:

KIRBY. Cosmic Carson's rocketship crashes on the outer ring of the galaxy. So the Solar Legion takes the drastic step of growing an android replica to take his place. Without Carson, the evil generals and the space pirates — they'll take over the entire galaxy! Only thing is, this new guy—he ain't a goody two-shoes. He may look like one on the outside, but inside—he's a brawler. A good-for-nothing street punk. But he's gotta keep up appearances, you know? Because he knows, no matter what his natural tendencies might be—it's the right thing to do.

IMMEDIATE FULL BLACKOUT.

END OF PLAY.

"It's the right thing to do." (Photo: Crystal Skillman)

COMMENTARY
by Fred Van Lente

Scene 1.

This Sotheby's auction did in fact take place on June 18, 1994, with most of those pieces available, and they were sold at those prices (rounded up or down as the case may be). The total sale value of all the Kirby art was $142,309.00.

The list of art and final prices is on pp26-7 of *The Collected Jack Kirby Collector Volume One* (John Morrow, ed.) Raleigh, NC: TwoMorrows, 1999. References to the Collected Jack Kirby Collector will hereafter be abbreviated to "CJKC" [volume number]:[page number]. Ergo, the reference above would read CJKC 1:26-7.

Scene 2.

Jack Kirby's childhood is most vividly evoked in a short, unfinished comics story he wrote and drew late in his career called "Street Code," which is reprinted in *Streetwise: Autobiographical Stories by Comic Book Professionals* (Jon B. Cooke and John Morrow, Eds.) Raleigh, NC: TwoMorrows Publishing, 2000. 14-23. See also Kirby biography in "Lord of Light" promotional package, CJKC 2:102-3. Ken Viola. "Jack Kirby: Master of Comic Book Art." CJKC 1:130-1.

This play originally began life as a biography of Kirby I worked on in 1999/2000 but ultimately abandoned. During that period Eric Evans and Gary Groth of *The Comics Journal* very kindly provided me with a copy of the raw transcript of Groth's 1989 interview with Jack and Rosalind ("Roz") Kirby. The comprehensive interview covers most of Kirby's life and career and filled in many gaps in the artist's early years.

"Cosmic Carson" was actually a Fox Features Syndicate house strip. The story quoted here was written and drawn by a young Jack as a completely different story; Joe Simon asked him to retrofit this pre-existing strip as a Carson story, where it appeared in the May 1940 issue of Fox's *Science Comics*. The Dispatcher and Spaceman's lines come directly from that tale, which I got from *The Complete Jack Kirby Vol. 1* (ed. Greg Theakston) Atlanta: Pure Imagination, 1997. A 1939 sci-fi strip, *Solar Legion*, which he created for TEM Publishing, was the writer/artist's first use of the pen name "Jack Kirby".

Despite Kirby's frequent claims later in life to have gotten into Pratt, when I inquired the university had no record of his ever having attended or enrolling there.

Scene 3.

Anyone interested in Fleischer Studios should check out Leslie Cabarga's excellent *The Fleischer Story* (De Capo Press 1998). The gory details of the strike come from stories in the May 6-7, 1937 *New York Times*.

Kirby would claim (CJKC 2:112, for example) to have left Fleischer Studios a few months before the 1937 strike, but also always gives as the primary reason for his leaving (CJKC 2:15, et al) their relocation to Miami, which happened almost a full year later. Also in CJKC 2:15, however, Kirby says that "it's fortunate I didn't go [to Florida] because soon after [the studio] moved, they all went on strike and men were laid off."

I am operating on the assumption that while in later life Kirby mistakenly believed that the strike and the move were coterminous occurrences, events did indeed unfold more or less as we present them in this story.

Scene 4.

The legendarily colorful Mr. Fox is vividly portrayed in Joe Simon's autobiography (co-written with his son Jim Simon) *The Comic Book Makers* (Crestwood II 1990). Fox's character also comes from interviews with other people who worked with him, most notably the artist Pierce Rice (*The Comics Journal* #219. January 2000: 86).

All of Simon's subsequent attempts to regain the copyright to Captain America (see below) say he had designed and named the hero before he ever brought Kirby onto the project.

The "Pants!" toast was inspired by the wonderful introduction Joe Simon wrote to the Marvel reprint of he and Kirby's *Fighting American* comics in the 1990s.

Scene 5.

Yes, Stan Lee/Stanley Lieber, according to several sources (particularly Simon), did actually play the flute in the office.

The pro-Nazi threats against Timely were quite real, and it was Kirby, not Simon, who received the lamppost threat in particular (CJKC 1:181). According to Simon's *Comic Book Makers,* the threats got so bad that Mayor Fiorello La Guardia had to provide Timely Comics with police protection for a time.

The Goldsteins actually lived above the Kurtzbergs, not the other way around, but reversing it makes more sense visually for the audience.

When it comes to who ratted Simon & Kirby out to Martin Goodman, Simon said, in a 2000 interview, "Stan said he didn't do it. Jack said, 'The next time I see that little son-of-a-bitch,

I'm gonna kill him.' And then, the next thing I knew[3], he went back to work for them, so what do what you gotta do, right?" (*Jack Kirby Collector* #25, downloaded from TwoMorrows web site 4/14/00.)

Patton's complaints about Alsace-Lorraine come directly from a letter of his from *The Patton Papers: 1940-1945* (Martin Blumenson, ed.) Boston: Houghton Mifflin, 1974.

Scene 6.

By all accounts, Kirby loved his war stories. The meat of the ones dramatized here come from Ray Wyman, Jr. "Jack Kirby on: World War II Influences." *The Jack Kirby Collector* #27. February 2000: 16-23; 1989 Groth interview; Greg Theakston. "Kirby's War." *Jack Kirby Quarterly*. Spring 1999: 6-13.

For the German language assist, many thanks to Timothy McCown Reynolds and Professor Johanna Vandrey of Northern Illinois University. (Love ya, Auntie Jo!)

Scene 7.

The mural, the work situation and the creation of *Young Romance* may be found in the Simons' *Comic Book Makers.*

Roz Kirby discusses her brief inking career, meeting Jack, and their life together in a lengthy 1995 interview with John Morrow that was a huge inspiration for this play in CJKC 2:40-51.

Scene 8.

Wertham's dialogue comes directly from the transcript of his Senate testimony. According to David Hadju's wonderful book about the crisis, *Ten Cent Plague* (Farrar, Straus and Giroux

---

[3] "Next thing I knew" = More than a decade later

2008), Kirby and Simon watched the televised hearings together.

Maybe it's just me, but I always detect a degree of condescension, in a big-brother sort of way, when Simon writes or talks about Kirby. The friction and conflict depicted in the play derives from that inference.

Scene 9.

This scene, and the next, are told through the eyes of the characters, of course. I did a less "biased" version of this tale in *The Comic Book History of Comics* (IDW 2012) with my longtime partner in crime, cartoonist Ryan Dunlavey. Later in life, both Lee and Kirby would claim, at various times, sole authorship of the Marvel Universe — Kirby most notoriously in the 1989 Groth interview of which I have the unedited transcript.

There Kirby claims, "Marvel was on its ass, literally, and when I came around, they were practically hauling out the furniture. They were literally moving out the furniture. They were beginning to move, and Stan Lee was sitting there crying. I told them to hold everything, and I pledged that I would give them the kind of books that would up their sales and keep them in business, and that was my big mistake."

However, Lee's two-page synopsis of *Fantastic Four #1* still exists; I've seen it. The resulting comic is considerably different, however. Applying Occam's Razor, one can assume this is due to Kirby's contributions. In the 1989 passage above Kirby is only a few months away from resolving the rancorous battle to get his artwork back and inclined to score-settle, perhaps.

Just so there's no ambiguity here, I will say unequivocally that Lee was an integral part of Marvel Comics' success, from the irreverent tone of his dialogue to his role as professional pitchman.

That said, the bulk of the creative "work," including the creation of major plot lines and characters, was undertaken by Jack Kirby, Steve (*Spider-Man, Dr. Strange*) Ditko, and other artistic collaborators. This seems to me almost self-evident, as a point of logic, if for no other reason than Lee's most fertile creative period came when he was working with Kirby and Ditko. Both those artists went on to continue to create beloved, long-lived characters without Lee (and Kirby, in particular, had had a long career of doing that before joining Marvel) and Lee's primary accomplishments since the 1960s have been *Striperella* and a Kardashian-esque meta-fame deriving from movie cameos.

Did Lee do nothing? Of course not. He wrote the words, after the drawing was completed. He was integral.

Is he reaping far more fame and credit than he deserves? Is it right the general pubic believes he is solely responsible, and, in many, many cases *drew* all those comics?

That judgment I'll leave up to you, True Believer.

Scene 10.

Longtime Kirby-watchers will recognize something familiar about this scene, in that it is mostly derived from an infamous profile of Marvel in general and Stan Lee in particular, by *New York Herald* reporter Nat Freedland: "Super-Heroes with Super Problems." (*The New York Herald Tribune Sunday Magazine.* January 9, 1966. Reprinted CJKC 4:156). The resulting article, with its "Assistant Foreman at a Girdle Factory" portrayal of Kirby, was, by many accounts, the final nail in the coffin of the relationship between the two men. Roy Thomas, Lee's assistant, who was called in to witness the same session the reporter observed, reports on Kirby being upset about it — and that even Stan himself was embarrassed by how over the top it came out — in an interview in CJKC 4:148.

The earlier opening with the college students was inspired by a different article later in the year, "OK, You Passed the 2-S Test —Now You're Smart Enough for Comic Books" (*Esquire*. September 1966: 115). It's worth noting that this article, one of the earliest mainstream pieces on Marvel, describes Stan Lee as "the **author** of Marvel's ten super-hero comics" (emphasis mine) and though Jack Kirby provides the illustrations for the tongue-in-cheek piece, his name (other than his signature on his art), or Ditko's, or any other artist's, is not mentioned anywhere in the article.

For all his obfuscating grandstanding, it's worth noting that Stan Lee himself gives Kirby's version of how the Silver Surfer was created in his own book *Son of Origins* (Fireside 1975).

(Roz on the Lee/Kirby working process: "I think they talked two minutes on the phone, and then Jack would go off and write the story on the side of the art." [Groth transcript])

The confrontation between Simon and Kirby over Simon's attempts to get the rights to Captain America back in the late 1960s is (not counting the dream sequence confrontation between Lee and Kirby, of course), the play's primary instance of pure speculation. According to *Comic Book Makers,* Goodman summoned Kirby into his office and claimed Simon was trying to backstab him, which is how he got Kirby to sign away Cap's rights so quickly (I'm not sure I've ever heard Kirby tell his side of this particular story). Our version aims to dramatize both the difference between the two men and Kirby's lifelong aversion to confrontation, which, I've found, is rather endemic in the comic book industry, now as well as then.

It's worth noting Simon attempted to reclaim Captain America one more time, in 2000, though he settled out of court with Marvel.

Simon actually grew up in Rochester, then went to Syracuse for work, but I worry about making the audience keep track of too many proper names, and "sipping tea in Syracuse" sounds better.

Scene 11.

Jack Kirby's legal troubles with Marvel Comics, over Joe Simon and his art, are ably summarized by John Morrow in "Art vs. Commerce" (*The Jack Kirby Collector* #24. April 1999: 28-31).

We also depended on contemporary articles for this scene, particularly Tom Heintjes' "The Negotiations: Jack Kirby discusses his efforts to retrieve his art from Marvel Comics" *The Comics Journal* #105 (February 1986). The complete text of the agreement Marvel originally wanted Kirby to sign may be found on the inside front cover of that issue of the *Journal*.

Kirby was the first Guest of Honor at the first official San Diego Comic-Con in August 1970.

Scene 12.

The fan who drove ten hours from Chicago went to AcmeCon '85 in Greensboro, North Carolina (CJKC 1: 193).

Crystal Skillman is the award-winning author of *Wild* (IRT Theater/SanguineTheatre in NYC; Kid Brooklyn Productions in Chicago); *Geek* (Vampire Cowboys/Incubator Arts, NYT and TONY Critics Pick); *Cut* (The Management, New York Times Critic's Pick); *The Vigil or The Guided Cradle* (ITG/The Brick Theater, NYIT Award Outstanding Play), *Drunk Art Love* (First Breath Reading Series, finalist for Harold Clurman Residency), and *Another Kind of Love.*

Her work has been seen Off Broadway at the Lucille Lortel Theater, as part of MCC Theater's Playlab series, and in the UK at Southwark Theater with Kibo Productions. She is co-writer with composer Bobby Cronin on the musical comedy *The Concrete Jungle* and also at work with Cronin on the musical adaptation of the film *Mary and Max,* with director Stafford Arima.

Fred Van Lente first became known for the *New York Times* bestsellers *Incredible Hercules, Marvel Zombies,* and *Cowboys & Aliens,* the basis for the feature film, as well as the American Library Association- and Xeric Award-winning *Action Philosophers.*

His other comics include the Harvey Award-nominated *Archer & Armstrong, The Comic Book History of Comics, Taskmaster, X Men Noir, The Amazing Spider-Man* and *Resurrectionists.*

Made in the USA
Charleston, SC
07 October 2014